A BEGINNER'S GUIDE TO

A Modern Introduction to Paganism for Beginners and New Seekers to Discover Earth-Centered Religions Through Nature-Based Spirituality

ELENA SHELBY

© **Copyright** 2020 - All rights reserved.

The content contained within this book may not be reproduced, duplicated or transmitted without direct written permission from the author or the publisher.

Under no circumstances will any blame or legal responsibility be held against the publisher, or author, for any damages, reparation, or monetary loss due to the information contained within this book, either directly or indirectly.

Legal Notice:

This book is copyright protected. It is only for personal use. You cannot amend, distribute, sell, use, quote or paraphrase any part, or the content within this book, without the consent of the author or publisher.

Disclaimer Notice:

Please note the information contained within this document is for educational and entertainment purposes only. All effort has been executed to present accurate, up to date, reliable, complete information. No warranties of any kind are declared or implied. Readers acknowledge that the author is not engaged in the rendering of legal, financial, medical or professional advice. The content within this book has been derived from various sources. Please consult a licensed professional before attempting any techniques outlined in this book.

By reading this document, the reader agrees that under no circumstances is the author responsible for any losses, direct or indirect, that are incurred as a result of the use of the information contained within this document, including, but not limited to, errors, omissions, or inaccuracies.

TABLE OF CONTENTS

INTRODUCTION 1
CHAPTER 1: WHAT IS PAGANISM? 9
   Glossary of Pagan Terms 10
   The Shared Characteristics of Pagan Paths 12
   Common Myths About Paganism and Pagans 16
   The History of Religion and the Birth of Paganism 20
   Paganism and the Law 24
   Paganism and Science 28
CHAPTER 2: PAGANISM IN MODERN SOCIETY 30
   So, How Many Pagans Are There Really and Where Do They Live? 30
   How Paganism Has Influenced Our Modern Traditions (and Why It Matters) 32
CHAPTER 3: BELIEFS 40
   Beliefs That Are Common Among Pagan Religions 41
   The Pagan View of Self 44
   Guiding Behaviors 45
CHAPTER 4: MAJOR PAGAN PATHS AND THEIR TRADITIONS 51
   African Diasporic Religions 52
   Alexandrian Wicca 52
   Ásatrú 53

Assianism 54
Baltic Neopaganism 54
Celtic Wicca 55
Christian Wicca 56
Dianic Wicca... 56
Druidry 57
Eclectic Paganism (Making Your Own Path)...................... 58
Faery Faith.. 58
Faery Wicca 59
Gardnerian Wicca 60
Hedge Witchcraft 60
Hellenism 61
Italo-Roman Neopaganism... 63
Kemetism 65
Mexicayotl.. 65
Odinism.. 67
Rodnovery 67
Stregheria... 68

CHAPTER 5: DEITIES 70
Most Commonly Worshiped Pagan Deities...................... 70
How to Engage a Deity 87
Pagan Views on the Devil and Angels 89
Is Paganism Compatible With Christianity? 91

CHAPTER 6: MAGIC(K) 93
Different Types of Magick 93
Tools of the Trade 100
The Rule of Three and Other Pitfalls of Magick 104

CHAPTER 7: RITUALS... 106

 Calling the Corners (and the Role of the Elements).......... 107

 Pagan Practices and Procedures 109

 Rituals for Beginners 112

CHAPTER 8: WHEEL OF THE YEAR 116

 Important Dates on the Wheel of the Year 116

 Personal Seasons 122

CHAPTER 9: CONTINUING YOUR SPIRITUAL JOURNEY 123

CHAPTER 10: CONTINUING YOUR PAGAN EDUCATION 129

 How Do I Continue My Education? 130

CONCLUSION 134

REFERENCES 136

INTRODUCTION

Witches! For centuries, this word has been screeched in horror or roared in damnation. Normally, it's being directed at a practitioner on a Pagan path, but that doesn't mean that Paganism deserves its darker reputation. One could argue that Paganism's reputation has been purposefully besmirched by the world's major Abrahamic religions in an attempt to discredit it. Why would you want to discredit the oldest type of religion known to mankind? I can't seem to think of any reason other than that Paganism is probably seen as a threat to the more restrictive, judgmental, and controlling modern mainstream religions.

If you've picked up this book, you've likely felt drawn to nature and nature-centric religions for quite some time, although it's likely that you haven't been sure how to accommodate this affinity within our modern society. Luckily, Paganism presents you with the opportunity to hone your powers while belonging to one of the fastest-growing communities in the world. Heathenism is making a comeback and with good reason! The Earth has slowly been dying at the hands of humankind for hundreds of years, it's high-time that those who are called to the path step up to the plate to bring balance back into the world.

The word 'Paganism' actually has two accepted definitions. Originally, it was used to describe any religion that wasn't classified as 'Christian,' although in modern times it has taken on a new meaning. These days it is generally used to refer to nature-centric religions like Wicca and Ásatrú or self-adapted religious practices that draw inspiration from pre-Christian religions. Etymologically, it is rooted in the Latin word 'pāgānus,' which means both 'rural' and 'civilian,' a fitting origin considering the value of the countryside to someone who feels most grounded when they're surrounded by as natural a setting as possible (like Pagans usually do).

Those who are drawn to Paganism are usually people who feel an intimate connection to nature, although there are a myriad of reasons why any one of the various Pagan paths might appeal to someone. Unlike Abrahamic religions, Paganism offers explanations for paranormal or supernatural events to those who have experienced them (or who regularly experience them), it worships and recognizes the feminine divine (and consequently frees itself of patriarchal thinking), and it shuns the concept of sin (and hell for sinners). Paganism also offers those who are interested in crystal healing, animal communication, communicating with the spirit world, herbal medicine, and energy work a way to practice and improve their crafts—abilities that are often demonized by some of the more popular religions.

I can't imagine how anyone could stand in a forest without hearing the trees whisper, touch a stone without feeling what it has seen, or stare into the eyes of a cat without being moved. How could anyone, seeing the splendor of the natural world, not want to embark on a Pagan path to becoming one with it? The modern world so often robs us of our connection with nature by keeping our eyes glued firmly to a screen and our backsides glued firmly to some office chair, but Paganism offers us a chance to reclaim our power by reconnecting with its source. To a Pagan, every bird song is a prayer, every babbling brook a hymn, every sunrise and sunset a sermon, every dewdrop holy water, and every spring blossom a verifiable miracle. The world is a more beautiful, more meaningful place through the eyes of a Pagan.

Paganism has seen a resurgence in modernity despite the Church's best attempts to wipe it out entirely during the dark ages. This conflict originally stemmed from the politics of the time as monarchs fought to maintain their power in a world that was more readily rejecting the idea of absolute authority. Back then, using the Church to control the minds of the people was the best way to keep the throne. Monarchs managed to weaponize Christianity by imprinting the idea of "The Diving Right of Kings," on the minds of their subjects. This doctrine proclaimed that kings were chosen by God to rule their people and that insubordination towards the king was a direct act of rebellion against God. Pagans were not so easily convinced that tyrants deserved to rule, which means that they were immediately seen as a threat to the status quo.

Modern pagans are once again redefining and challenging societal norms by creating a space that is inclusive, wholesome, and humanitarian in a world that is forever trying to convince people that their authentic-selves are not good enough. Paganism offers a safe space for those who are looking to belong and a community for those who can feel the quiet power of the Earth flowing through them, regardless of what they may look like, their gender, their race, their age, their sexual preferences (or lack thereof), their social or their financial status.

It is perhaps because of Pagans' naturally empathetic and charismatic nature that so many of the ancient world's revolutionary leaders who managed to rally thousands (if not hundreds of thousands) of people behind them identified as such, even when the world was starting to push them to convert to one of the two main Abrahamic religions: Christianity or Islam. Examples of such Pagan folk heroes are Boudica, Gwenc'hlan, Sexred, Porphyry of Tyre, Julian, and Hypatia.

Boudica is the most well-known of the lot. She was a Celtic queen who ruled as the sole monarch of her people for a period during the first century AD. She was whipped and forced to watch her daughters being sexually assaulted by Roman soldiers (the same Roman soldiers who were intent on forcing Christianity on all of the territories that they conquered by brute force) during an insurrection. She refused to let her people be yoked into a foreign religion and be physically violated. She mounted an offense that saw her personally charging into battle alongside her subjects, an act of bravery that the Romans had not expected from a woman.

Unfortunately, her efforts were doomed from the start, despite her faith that the Gods would lend a helping hand; the Roman troops outnumbered the indigenous Celts one-hundred to one. After a battle with Paulinus's troops, Boudica's troops were brutally defeated, and, fearing capture, she chose to drink a vial of poison rather than let herself be taken by the Romans. Her story has been told and retold for nearly 2,000 years, possibly making her the most famous Pagan ruler to ever have lived.

Gwenc'hlan was a Breton poet and bard who was much beloved by his fans (a group of people that was allegedly made up of anyone who had ever heard him sing). He held on to his Pagan beliefs even though Christianity had become the dominant religion and wasn't afraid to sing or write about the Gods and doctrines that he so strongly believed in. His devotion eventually cost him dearly as he was arrested for spreading Pagan ideologies in the late sixth century and consequently had his eyes gouged out as punishment for his transgressions.

Sexred was a Saxon king who was born to Christian parents. His Christian upbringing did not stop him from developing an affinity for the original Pagan beliefs of the region. He soon abolished all of the rules in his kingdom that prohibited the public practice of Pagan traditions and religions and started encouraging his subjects to retake their Pagan beliefs.

Porphyry of Tyre, the ancient Roman philosopher, was one of the world's first proponents of ethical vegetarianism. When he wasn't busy writing philosophy books on animal rights, he was busy writing them about Roman Paganism. He passionately believed that the Romans should remain loyal to the old Gods, instead of embracing the new—even going as far as challenging the historical accuracy of the Christian Bible. Luckily, his influence spared him from suffering the same fate as some of the most passionate Pagans of the time suffered. His academic work on the philosophical merits of ethical vegetarianism is studied in University courses all around the world, even though he died about 1,600 years ago.

Hypatia was the first female mathematician and one of the first figureheads of the feminist movement. She lived in Alexandria in the fourth century and shared her vast mathematical knowledge with hundreds of new students every year for most of her life. Despite being passionately Pagan, she loved all of her students regardless of their religious orientation. A trait that was unique during a time that was known for its growing religious tensions. She was brutally murdered for her beliefs, by a mob of Christians in 415 AD, despite her tolerance towards their beliefs.

Of course, influential Pagans still exist in modernity too, they're just generally less recognized for their beliefs.

Erich Friedrich Wilhelm Ludendorff was a general during World War I who was responsible for leading the German troops to victory during the battles of Tannenberg and Liège. While it certainly can't be said that Ludendorff was a good person (in fact, he's probably best described as pure evil), he was certainly a decent leader—inspiring unbelievable bravery in the men that served under him (probably because they were terrified of him). In his writings, he attributed his military success to the worship of German Pagan Gods, paving the way for many German neo-pagans who would come after him.

Erich Ludendorff married a remarkable woman named Mathilde Friederike Karoline Ludendorff (originally Spiess) in 1925. Mathilde was an accomplished psychiatrist who specialized in gender-specific anatomical differences in the human brain. Despite her gendered approach to her studies, she was a firm feminist and asserted the importance of women's rights and gender equality during a time in which the political majority in Germany did not support this view. Mathilde was raised by her father, a Lutheran priest, but abandoned the Lutheran church in 1913, choosing instead to invest her faith in the German Gods of old.

Neopaganism isn't just reserved for German academics and generals, though. It has seen a surge in popularity all around the world in recent years. There have even been celebrities who have embraced the Path in recent years.

Raimonds Vējonis, who served as the president of Latvia for one term between 2015 and 2019, is a self-professed Baltic Pagan. He focused most of his efforts on environmental protection during his presidency, just as one might expect a Pagan president to do.

Dylan Sprouse, an American actor who is best known for his roles in *The Suite Life of Zack and Cody* and *The Suite Life on Deck*, announced in 2017 that he was a practicing Pagan and went as far as referring to himself as a 'heathen.'

One of the founders of the Gay Activist Alliance was a Wiccan priest. His name was Leo Martello, and he was drawn to Gardnerian Wicca because it was one of the few spiritual paths that he was aware of that did not shun his lifestyle or call it a sin. His Roman Catholic upbringing had led to him falling out of love with traditional religious practices and his experiences in a Catholic boarding school seemed to seal the deal. He was a committed member of the Wiccan community until he passed away in 2000.

Will you be the next person to take up the mantle? Your journey down a Pagan Path may lead you to many wonderful places that would have otherwise remained inaccessible to you. It may grant you powers beyond your wildest dreams, introduce you to important antagonists in your life, help you to overcome trauma or adversity, assist you in achieving your dreams, and give you a community to belong to.

CHAPTER 1
WHAT IS PAGANISM?

You can't understand something if you don't understand its origins. It's easier to know what fruit a tree will bear when you know which seed was planted. Your new journey on your chosen Pagan path will be no different. Understanding the influencing factors behind the Path that resonates with you most will not only help you to better understand your Path, but it will help you to better understand yourself and your internal motivations too. This chapter will serve as a guide to the roots and origins of Pagan belief systems.

As was briefly touched on during the introduction, Paganism has a dual definition. However, for the purposes of this book, the word 'Pagan,' should be assumed to refer to the practice of a nature-centric belief system or the incorporation of some of its principles into a self-adapted belief system. There are several terms that you'll need to come to grips with during your exploration of Pagan belief systems, although you should find dealing with them relatively easy once you've fully immersed yourself in your chosen Path.

Glossary of Pagan Terms

Altar: An altar is usually a table, countertop, shelf, or other flat surface that a Pagan dedicates to a specific deity or uses to practice magick. Altars usually display important tools of the trade like a practitioner's mortar and pestle, colored candles, divination materials like tarot cards or crystal balls, and amulets.

Amulets: Amulets are objects that are imbibed with some kind of protective power. They lend their capabilities to their wearers, shielding them from misfortune and misadventures alike. In certain Pagan traditions, amulets can be created using magick, although they're also regularly found in nature in the form of specific kinds of crystals.

Athame: A ritualistic dagger (usually blunt) used during certain

Pagan belief systems' magickal traditions.

Balefire: A bonfire that has been created for the purpose of incorporating it in a Pagan ritual or an act of magick.

Book of Shadows: Many Pagan belief systems, including Wicca, encourage their practitioners to keep a journal known as the Book of Shadows. This book contains information about any rituals or spells which the practitioner may have participated in and notes their relative outcomes. Pagans use their Book of Shadows to gather information and to reflect on past practices.

Crystallomancy: The act of predicting the future by 'reading' or interpreting crystals.

Faeries: Not to be confused with 'fairies.' Faeries are powerful Earth spirits that are not to be messed with. Certain Pagan paths incorporate communicating with Faeries (sometimes called 'the Fey') into their spiritual paths, although it is almost always reserved for more experienced practitioners.

Geomancy: The art of using stones, dirt, or dust to predict the future or ask for guidance.

Invocation: The act of calling up a spirit, entity, or deity and allowing it to take possession of your body for a specific purpose such as receiving a blessing from it or making use of its power during a ritual or ritual magick.

Magick: Most Pagan practitioners prefer using the term 'magick,' when referring to the elements of their beliefs that encourage divination and spell casting. 'Magick,' is preferred over the term, 'magic,' because it differentiates magickal Pagan rituals from slide-of-hand and magic as it is portrayed by Hollywood and the media.

Necromancy: The act of summoning the dead for assistance during ritual spell work or divination. Numerous Pagan belief systems incorporate some form of necromancy in their traditions.

Numerology: The art of predicting the future using randomly drawn or chosen numbers.

Runes: This word is normally used to refer to letters from the ancient Nordic alphabet. They're usually inscribed on stones or sticks and then used during divination rituals.

Scrying: The act of staring into a mirror for prolonged periods to divine the future.

Talisman: A talisman is a crystal, stone, jewelry piece, piece of clothing, or other item that has been magickally imbued with properties that allow it to attract a specific kind of energy. Pagan practitioners employ talismans to attract everything from love to money.

The Shared Characteristics of Pagan Paths

Although there are hundreds of Pagan paths, from Hellenism to Afro-centric Paganism, they all seem to share a handful of common characteristics that make their ethoses so similar that any other differences in belief or tradition seem almost negligible. These shared characteristics are nature-centricity, blessedness, humanitarianism, the belief in karma, polytheism, and clergy.

Nature-Centricity

All Pagan belief systems are based on nature worship. This is not to say that all Pagans worship the earth, sun, and moon, but rather that all Pagan belief systems draw their inspiration from a deep respect for the earth, nature, and natural cycles.

Natural cycles (from moon phases to reproductive cycles) are revered in most, if not all, Pagan religions. This is one of the characteristics that sets Paganism apart from Abrahamic belief systems which are often only concerned with one cycle: That of birth and death.

The inherent nature-centricity of Pagan belief systems is also obvious when considering the connection that most Pagan deities have with certain natural elements. For example, Poseidon, the God of the sea, and Selene, the Goddess of the moon.

Many Pagan belief systems also posit that their practitioners can learn how to harness the energies and powers of nature, and influence them to change the world around them.

Blessedness

If you've ever met a practicing Pagan, you've probably heard the phrase, "Blessed be." "Blessed be," is a common greeting or acknowledgment in Pagan circles and it's reflective of most Pagan belief systems' approach to others.

Pagans are far more concerned with imparting good energy on those who they encounter than they are in influencing the world for their own benefit or seeking retribution through harnessing the Earth's power. It is because of this that talismans, amulets, and protective spells are so popular among Pagan magick practitioners, while harmful spells are largely undocumented and unsupported by the community.

Not only are many Pagan belief systems occupied with the idea that blessing others also holds value for the blesser themselves, but they also often encourage their followers to seek blessings from others like their fellow practitioners, their honored deities, their familiars, spirits, elementals, and other entities. While a blessing from a fellow Pagan might offer you protection from negative energies or those who wish to do you harm, a blessing from a deity like Poseidon or Selene has the potential to magnify your natural abilities, allowing you to bend the world to your will armed with nothing but the intention to do so.

Humanitarianism/Humanism

There's a reason why the classical depiction of a witch is an old, wise medicine woman living in a cottage in the forest, healing the nearby villagers' ills despite being ostracized and criticized by them. Pagans have been serving the communities around them since the dawn of time, using their knowledge of herbs, crystals, and energy to aid those that need their help.

Pagan belief systems tend to have strong humanitarian elements. In some ways, these elements stem from the concept of blessedness and the idea that blessing others could be beneficial to yourself in the long run too, although it could be argued that it is Pagans' inherent respect for nature that drives them to respect the sanctity of life, and thus endeavor to improve the lives of those around them.

Most Pagan belief systems urge their followers to be good to those that they encounter on their Path (or at the very least not to do any harm to them—as the Wiccan rede states, "If you harm none, do what you will.")

The Belief in Karma

All Pagan belief systems posit that your actions come back to you in some way or another. Some Pagan belief systems state that your actions during this life impact the kind of life you'll have in the next or during your next reincarnation, while others believe that your actions come back to you during this life in the form of, "The Rule of Three," (that was discussed in the Glossary on Pagan Terms) or a similar doctrine.

This belief in karmic retribution permeates Pagan culture and encourages Pagans to consider the effects that their actions have on others by making them aware of the fact that those effects are bound to ricochet and affect them in some way too.

Polytheism

'Polytheism,' means the belief in more than one God or deity. Most Pagan belief systems are polytheistic and encourage their followers to get to know their various Gods or deities before choosing one (or a few of them) to devote all of their praise, worship, and magickal involvement to. Unlike many mainstream religions, Pagan Gods don't seem to take offense if you don't choose to worship them which means that Pagans are free to only worship those deities that they resonate with.

Most Pagan belief systems have elaborate folktales to explain the significance and roles of their various deities. This means that beginners who are just starting their journey down a Pagan path may need to devote some time to get to know these accounts before they're able to start practicing in earnest.

Clergy

A lot of new Pagans are surprised to learn that most Pagan belief systems have some form of the clergy but it's entirely true. Although Pagan clergy do not perform the same functions as

Abrahamic clergy like popes, priests, and pastors do, they are an important part of their respective belief systems.

Pagan clergy take the form of coven leaders, practicing elders, high priests, and high priestesses. Their purpose is to facilitate rites, traditions, and rituals while assisting their members in following their paths.

Of course, not all Pagans belong to organized religious movements and that's okay too. No Pagan belief system condemns practicing in private or alone, although joining a Pagan community certainly holds many advantages (companionship possibly being the most pertinent).

Common Myths About Paganism and Pagans

Pagans have had to practice their traditions, religions, and rituals in secret for hundreds of years, so it's not surprising that the general public doesn't know much about them. This widespread unfamiliarity eventually led to the development of several misconceptions about this spiritual path and the people that follow it.

The First Myth: All Pagans Believe in the Same Thing

As was discussed earlier, 'Pagan' is a blanket term for many different religions and belief systems. Consequently, Pagans' beliefs often differ dramatically. These differences can be expressed in the way that they worship their deities, the deities that they worship, their idea of the afterlife, or even in their world view.

The common traits that all Pagan belief systems share are not dominant enough to ensure that they create uniformity. This can be observed in the differences in religious practices when comparing two Pagan belief systems to one another; a Wiccan's religious practices don't have much in common with a Hindu's religious practices.

However, it's important to remember that this diversity is exactly what makes Paganism the wonderful spiritual path that it is. There is no Pagan path that is better or superior to another. They're all equally valid. The most important tenet is to choose the path that resonates with you the most and to respect the paths that others have chosen.

The Second Myth: You Can't be a Pagan if You're a Christian, Muslim, or Jew

While this myth might be true in the semantic sense, it's not true in practice. Many Pagans identify as Christians, Jews, and Muslims by finding ways to reconcile their beliefs with their Pagan practices. Many hold that Paganism can supplement an Abrahamic religion without contradicting it, arguing that the principles of humanism, humanitarianism, karma, and blessedness found in Paganism compliment the mandates of their Christian, Jewish, or Muslim religious texts.

Every individual practitioner needs to decide for themselves whether they want to practice Paganism in conjunction with another religion or whether they'd like to embark on a fully Pagan path.

The Third Myth: All Pagans Practice Witchcraft

It's certainly true that a great number of Pagan belief systems incorporate magickal elements but that doesn't mean that all Pagans practice magick. Even those Pagans who are on a path that does allow or encourage its practitioners to dabble in magick aren't necessarily practicing it themselves. Many individuals choose to abstain for a variety of reasons while others simply aren't on a path that recognizes magick or the practice thereof.

Regardless, it's important to separate the idea of Pagan magick from *Harry Potter* style hocus-pocus in your mind. Pagan magick is usually built upon elaborate ritual rites and doesn't normally promise instantaneous results. Pagans aren't all on their way to Hogwarts to learn transfiguration and the image of Pagan pointy-hatted witches that the mainstream media perpetuates couldn't be further from the truth.

The Fourth Myth: Pagans Engage in Ritual Animal Sacrifice

Certain ancient Pagan belief systems did incorporate animal sacrifice in their rituals hundreds of years ago but so did Christianity, Judaism, and Islam. Animal sacrifice used to be rife across the entire religious spectrum. Luckily, it has become far less common in modernity. These days, very few Pagan paths encourage animal sacrifice, in fact, many of them actively discourage it by mandating a certain level of respect for the natural world and the creatures that inhabit it.

Over the years many entirely false stories and articles have been circulated around the web that claim that Pagans steal black cats for ritual sacrifice during Halloween or that they nab dogs out of their gardens to sacrifice them to some dark deity. Most (if not absolutely all) of these tales are entirely unsubstantiated and seem to have been promulgated with the sole purpose of causing division and hysteria.

Generally speaking, Pagans love animals just as much as anybody else would (if not more than most people would) so you certainly don't have to feel the need to hide Fluffy if you ever invite one over for tea.

The Fifth Myth: Pagans are Promiscuous

This myth surely came into existence because of Hollywood's insistence on portraying witches as naked women prancing about under the moon, leading men away from their Godly wives. Most Pagans enjoy a good old prance under the moon as much as the next person but very few of them actually do it naked.

The sexual element of some Pagan paths has largely been sensationalized by the media for the sake of selling movie tickets. Out of the thousands of Pagan paths in existence, two or three make mention of sexual practices during magickal rites, a ratio that would suggest that sexual traditions are the exception, not the rule, when it comes to Paganism.

Of course, that doesn't mean that Paganism is prudish or unaccepting when it comes to the concept of sex. Unlike many mainstream religions, Paganism generally doesn't encourage its followers to get married before engaging in sexual intercourse nor does it shame them for the kind or number of partners that they choose (as long as this partner, or these partners, are all consenting adults).

The History of Religion and the Birth of Paganism

Stonehenge, an ancient Pagan worship site located in England, was erected 3,000 years before the reported birth of Christ, the oldest surviving religious texts are ancient Egyptian manuals that have been carbon-dated to be approximately 4,400-years old, and the first account of the 'Great Flood' was written by Pagan Sumerians about 4,000-years ago. Considering all of this, it's pretty obvious that Paganism has been around for much longer than all of today's mainstream religions have. It could be said that human beings are Pagan by default, as that is the position that our earliest ancestors took and that we have to be taught and molded to follow other religious ideologies.

Historians believe that religion as we know it (in the form of human beings believing in and worshiping a higher power or higher powers) came into existence about 5,500 years ago in Sumer, a region of Mesopotamia. Early Sumerian beliefs were much less hierarchical than most modern belief systems are today since the Sumerians viewed themselves as being their Gods' equals, rather than their subjects or servants. This ideology was centered on the idea that human beings were created to labor alongside the Gods, instead of to labor for them. In return for their labor, the Sumerians believed that their Gods rewarded them by providing for them and by offering them protection. Although the entire range of ancient Sumerian Gods and Goddesses aren't known, scientists have been able to determine who the main deities of the time were. Ostensibly, it seems as if most of the Pagan worship taking place in ancient Sumer was directed at Marduk, Tiamat, Absu, and Inanna.

Absu was the ancient Sumerian God of freshwater and Tiamat

ruled over saltwater. According to legend, Absu amalgamated his freshwater with Tiamat's salty oceans and the turmoil created by the unnatural mixture birthed the rest of the original Sumerian Gods and Goddesses. Marduk was known as the "Shepherd of Gods," because of his mandate to maintain order among the rest of the deities.

The Sumerians believed that Marduk fought an epic battle against Tiamat, who was intent upon unleashing chaos upon the human world and defeated him, thus allowing human civilization to flourish because of the ensuing orderly nature of the material world. Inanna (known as Ishtar to later civilizations) was the Sumerian Goddess of sex, sex workers, fertility, and war (quite an impressive resumé). While some prayed to her for guidance on political matters or protection in battle, others asked her to help them conceive and inversely even relied on her to keep unwanted pregnancies at bay.

The ancient Sumerians believed that all people, regardless of the kind of lives that they led during their time on Earth, went to the same place after they died. According to their religious texts, the souls of the dead were thought to travel to a cavern hundreds of miles beneath the Earth's surface where they spent the rest of eternity feasting on dirt. While eating dirt in a cavern doesn't do well when compared to the promise of the Pearly Gates, it's important to remember that the Sumerians experienced religion in its infancy and were probably more than happy to accept any afterlife over the idea that one might not exist at all.

The Egyptians were hot on the Sumerians' heels. Some historians claim that religion in Ancient Egypt may have predated religion in Sumer even though the ancient Egyptian religious texts that have been discovered have been dated to be one to two hundred years younger than those that were discovered in Sumerian ruins.

Although religion in Egypt largely developed independently of religion in Sumer, the two belief systems share some striking similarities. The ancient Egyptians also believed that the world was born from a stormy body of water that birthed the primordial mound (the first bit of inhabitable ground), the air, the sun, and the wind. The main difference between the beliefs of the ancient Egyptians and those of the Sumerians is their idea of the afterlife. While Sumer's afterlife seems like some primitive version of hell, Egypt's afterlife is closer to what most modern people would like to imagine it to be like. The Egyptians called this afterlife the "Field of Reeds." Their religious texts indicate that they believed that the Field of Reeds was identical to the material world in every way imaginable to create the perfect world for the soul that had to inhabit it.

The Middle East and Africa weren't the only continents that experienced their first Pagan stirrings about 5,000 years ago, India saw the birth of Hinduism around this time too. Hinduism is a form of Paganism regardless of how you view it. It's a religion that is entirely centered on the idea of humanism, blessedness, the belief in karma, and is largely nature-centric. It also fulfills the requirement of being polytheistic as it recognizes approximately 330 million different Gods and Goddesses.

Hinduism revolves around the concept that the supreme being, Brahma, has divided himself into millions of minor deities to make his existence more comprehensible to us mere mortals. Hindus strive to be reunited with Brahma by improving their karmic balance. Those who haven't been able to improve their karma enough to be reunited with the supreme being are reincarnated over and over again until they can do so.

The Americas saw several different brands of Paganism evolving alongside their indigenous peoples, the most interesting of which probably belonged to the Mayans. The Mayan empire was nothing to scoff at. It covered large areas of land in countries that are now known as Guatemala, Belize, and Mexico about 4,000 years ago. The Mayans' belief system is best described as animistic. They believed that all things, animate and inanimate, had a certain 'sacredness' about them known as k'uh. This inherent sacredness meant that all things had to be treated with a certain measure of respect.

The Mayans believed that the Gods (they recognized about 250 of them) created human beings in the form of four men and four women by mixing dough made out of yellow maize with their blood. As the story goes, these four men and four women soon grew too wise, so wise that the Gods felt threatened by their knowledge. Seeing his fellow deities become jealous of the humans, and growing concerned that they may opt to destroy them for the sake of their egos, Huracán (the God of the heavens) created a great mist in the minds of men, saving them from the other Gods' wrath, but robbing them of their godlike wisdom.

The Mayan afterlife was a pleasant place, but you had to travel through Xibalba to get there. Xibalba is essentially hell. It's a dangerous place filled with demons, peril, and pain that the undead had to navigate on their journey to the afterlife. The only souls that were exempt from having to travel through Xibalba were the souls of those who had committed suicide, who had died in battle, or who had died during childbirth.

Although many early Pagan religions and beliefs have been lost to the sands of time, many others form the foundations of neo-pagan practices and other nature-centric belief systems that have seen a resurgence in modern times. It's also interesting to observe the similarities and differences in early Pagan religions. While it's obvious that the idea of the world being born from a turbulent body of water seemed prevalent at the time, it's also ostensibly true that there doesn't seem to have been much consensus on what the afterlife was supposed to be like. While many early civilizations hoped it would be a pleasant place fashioned after an ideal world, an equal amount thought that it was probably a dreary place with little opportunity for anything other than amplified eternal suffering.

Paganism and the Law

"What impact does the law have on Paganism?" you might be wondering. The answer is, "Actually, quite a bit." Especially if you're not lucky enough to live in a country that has decriminalized it. Being a practicing Pagan, especially one that engages in any kind of magick, is a high-risk activity in certain countries. Some countries' approach to regulating witchcraft is pretty laughable, like the ban on irresponsible broomstick riding that is still on Swaziland's rule books. This law states that witches are not allowed to pilot their broomsticks at altitudes of greater than 492 feet above the ground.

Unfortunately, not all countries are so accommodating when it comes to the Pagans that they perceive to be witches. In 2009, Dubai enacted legislation that allowed for the creation of an "Anti-Witchcraft Unit." Dubai's government even went as far as creating hotlines that citizens could use to report their neighbors if they suspected that they might be practicing magick or be involved in witchcraft. While you could be fined up to $50,000 for piloting your broomstick more than 492 feet above ground in Swaziland, you could get put to death for owning a crystal collection that's a little too elaborate for the government's liking in Dubai.

Swaziland's jolly acceptance of airborne witches has also sadly not rubbed off on all of the other countries belonging to the African Union. Nearly two-fifths of all criminal charges brought against civilians in the Central African Republic are based on allegations of witchcraft. These allegations are often made by jealous neighbors and scorned lovers but regularly lead to hefty prison sentences. The Central African Republic's juvenile courts are also laboring under the weight of the increased workload that witchcraft cases bring. Local news outlets report that up to one in every twenty cases heard by the juvenile courts in this country center on magic-related charges.

However, not all rules that might affect practicing Pagans are aimed at stopping them from utilizing their magickal abilities. In 2011, Romania enacted legislation that now allows the government to require certain magickal professionals, like astrologers, tarot card readers, mediums, psychics, witches, and fortune-tellers, to pay taxes on the income they receive from the magickal services that they render. Although nobody enjoys having to pay taxes, having to pay them does give your chosen profession a certain sense of legitimacy that was not considered entirely unwelcome by the Romanian Pagan community.

While witchcraft is taxed, punished, or regulated in other countries, it's largely unrecognized by American and Canadian courts which means that Pagans are generally free to practice all aspects of their belief system in these countries without fear of repercussions. In the United States of America (USA), the First Amendment of the Constitution guarantees every American citizen the inalienable right to freedom of religion and the freedom to practice the religion of their choice. Canada's

Charter of Rights and Freedoms guarantees every Canadian citizen the same rights.

Canada's modern approach to religion doesn't mean that it doesn't still have some antiquated witchcraft laws on its books. An example of this is a Canadian criminal case that was brought before the court in 2018 which saw two women charged with the crime of "pretending to be witches" under the country's criminal code (specifically, section 365). Although the defendants certainly deserved to be charged with something for swindling their clients out of hundreds of thousands of dollars, many people were shocked that the prosecutors decided to charge them under such a medieval clause. However, it doesn't seem like this Canadian law will be recognized for much longer as the government is working hard to eliminate "zombie laws" (laws that are no longer applicable in modernity) from existing legislation.

While the USA no longer has any recognized legislation that allows its prosecutors to charge offenders with witchcraft-related charges, certain states have outlawed the act of telling fortunes, reading tarot cards, or divining the future for profit. However, the regional bans on the telling of fortunes for profit are seen as an anti-fraud measure rather than an attack on the Pagan or magickal community.

In modernity, American courts have readily sanctified the legitimacy of Pagan religions through an ever-growing base of supportive case law. Dettmer v. Landon was the most prolific court case ever heard in the USA that was centered around the rights of Pagans. It was heard in 1980 after the defendant, Mr. Dettmer, an inmate at a local penitentiary facility, sued the Director of the Virginia Department of Corrections; Mr. Landon. Dettmer was aggrieved because he was a practicing

Wiccan but had been denied access by the prison to the ritual daggers that he needed to perform common Wiccan rituals and ceremonies by the prison authorities.

Dettmer was successful in convincing the court that Wicca deserved to be treated with the same amount of reverence as Christianity and Islam are. The court supported this view and forever made it a part of the academic American legal landscape by commenting on it in its *obiter dictum*. Unfortunately for Dettmer, he did not succeed in convincing the court that an inmate should have access to knives, ritual or not. Even though Dettmer didn't achieve what he had set out to achieve, the ruling served as a landmark case and has ensured that Paganism receives the legal protection and recognition that it deserves. As one might imagine, Dettmer v. Landon set the stage for many cases centered around Pagan practices.

Twenty-nine years after Dettmer's case was heard, Merced v. Kasson was brought before a Fifth Circuit court. Mr. Merced was a Santeria (a form of Afro-Caribbean Paganism) priest who was stopped from performing a ritual animal sacrifice in his own home by the authorities. The City of Euless argued that they didn't stop Merced from completing the sacrifice on religious grounds but rather out of concern for public health and additional worries surrounding animal welfare. The court was having none of it and stated that, as the sacrifice was being performed in Merced's home, there was no risk to public health. The court ruled in Merced's favor, asserting that animal sacrifice couldn't be removed from Santeria's practices without fundamentally changing the religion.

Although Pagans often still face discrimination in the workplace and when dealing with law enforcement, it seems as though the judiciary's attitude towards magick and nature-centric religions are slowly changing for the better.

Paganism and Science

Many people shun Paganism as being nothing more than fairy tales and folklore, arguing that science simply doesn't support certain tenets of most nature-centric religions like the idea of animism. Consequently, you might be surprised to learn that science is increasingly taking a stance that seems to support many claims made by Pagan belief systems.

One of the elements of many Pagan religions that people struggle to believe in because they believe that science claims it to be impossible is magick. The fallacy in this kind of thinking is the fact that science doesn't claim that magick is impossible or unreal but rather that it has no basis to measure this kind of phenomenon.

In recent years, quantum mechanics has started offering up some unusual findings. The most notable of these was derived from an experiment that was conducted in 1998 called the "double-slit experiment." This scientific inquiry involved shining high-powered lasers through two tiny slits made in a solid wooden board with the idea that the pattern of light emerging on the other side would prove that light traveled in waves, rather than in particles.

What the scientists conducting the experiment observed (or rather, what they didn't observe) changed the way that we view reality forever. They realized that the light acted differently when it was being observed by a human being versus when it was simply being tracked. From this, they inferred that reality was materially 'changed' when it was being observed. This means that an observer fundamentally has the power to change the material world around them.

What does this mean for Paganism? Well, if you can change your immediate surroundings simply by looking at them, it increases the probability that more complicated magick is possible too.

Quantum physicists also believe that all matter, every atom in every molecule, is simply an expression of energy. That means that you're made up out of thousands of billions of little individual bundles of energy but it also means that you'll likely be able to change the nature of the things around you simply by directing your energy to influence them. That's a pretty awe-inspiring thought, isn't it? Especially when you consider the possibility that any number of Pagan paths might be able to teach you to do exactly that.

CHAPTER 2
PAGANISM IN MODERN SOCIETY

Pagan deities often get referred to as "the Old Gods," but that's not entirely true anymore. An unexpected Pagan revival seems to have swept across the globe in recent years, likely due to the ongoing battle to improve religious tolerance all around the world. This chapter will address the ever-changing Pagan demographics. We will also explore how the modern world has been influenced by Pagan beliefs, often in unexpected ways.

So, How Many Pagans Are There Really and Where Do They Live?

It's pretty difficult to gather any accurate data on how many Pagans there are worldwide because so many of them have to practice in secret to avoid being ostracized or even persecuted. Regardless of the insurmountability of the task, a few researchers have made some rather decent efforts at collecting as much data as they reliably can on the subject.

Most studies estimate that there are between three and six million admitted Pagans around the globe, although certain Christian institutions claim there are as many as ten million. Regardless of which number is correct, Pagans make up the smallest minority of the religious population.

These same studies approximate that this global Pagan population is made up of between one and five million admitted Wiccans, between 100,000 and half a million Hellens, 100,000 Rodnovers, one million Hetans, 800,000 Romuvans, 140,000 Taaraists, and 1.3 million people who simply identify as 'Pagan' or 'Neo-Pagan.'

Naturally, some countries have larger Pagan populations than others. Countries like the USA and the UK report alarmingly small Pagan populations, with no more than one or two percent of their populations identifying as such. However, certain European countries, like Armenia and Lithuania, report that up to a third of their population identifies as Pagan.

Interestingly, more women report identifying as Pagan than men do. More than 70% of Pagans are women. The reason for the gender discrepancy isn't entirely clear, although it's likely due to several factors like the fact that women are statistically more likely to be religious overall or that women are simply drawn to the idea of the Feminine Divine that Paganism offers (in stark contrast to the patriarchal structures of more mainstream religions).

How Paganism Has Influenced Our Modern Traditions (and Why It Matters)

Few people are aware of the immense influence that Paganism historically had on the modern world. Many of them regularly engage in Pagan traditions, practices, feasts, and holidays without even knowing it.

It wouldn't be a stretch to say that the world would be a very different place if Paganism hadn't influenced it in the way that it has, probably a much more boring place, too.

The Tooth Fairy

We all anxiously deposited our newly lost baby teeth under our pillows (or in our shoes in some countries) before we went to bed as kids. We knew that the morning would usher in the promise of a couple of coins (or a bill if we were lucky) in trade for our baby teeth, but how many of us know the tooth fairy's origin story?

You guessed right, the tooth fairy has its roots planted firmly in historic Pagan practices. Hundreds of years ago, Celtic Pagans encouraged their children to place their baby teeth under their pillows before going to bed. Just like modern parents, they snuck into their kids' rooms at night to retrieve them. Unlike modern parents, it wasn't something they did to give their child a dollar or two in exchange for the trauma of losing a tooth, it was integral to the child's survival.

Early Celtic Pagans believed that evil spirits would steal any baby teeth that were left lying around and use them to possess or curse the child who the teeth had originally belonged to. To ensure that this fate didn't befall their beloved offspring, they'd spirit away the hidden baby teeth in the middle of the night and dispose of them by burying them in an unmarked location or burning them.

Placing Your Hand in Front of Your Mouth When You Yawn

While it's simply good manners to put your hand in front of your mouth when you're yawning in modernity, the practice originated from a place of medical necessity rather than as a form of etiquette.

Roman Pagan doctors knew that babies were much more prone to dying mysterious deaths than toddlers, children, or adults were, but they weren't entirely sure why. Today we know that Sudden Infant Death Syndrome (SIDS) and birth defects are responsible for many seemingly inexplicable infant deaths; but back then it must have seemed as if something supernatural was at play. They started theorizing that perhaps babies died such inexplicable deaths because, unlike adults, they were incapable of covering their mouths when they yarned.

Adult Romans covered their mouths while yawning to stop their 'life essence' from leaking and escaping out of their mouths but babies were unable to do so, which meant that one yawn too many could mean the end of a baby. Luckily, today we know that yawning doesn't endanger your "life essence," but the practice has stuck around nonetheless.

Bridesmaids

In modernity, bridesmaids are often clothed in dresses that

differ in color from the bride's wedding dress. I mean, what kind of modern bride wants her bridesmaids to show up to her wedding looking just like her? However, this wasn't always the case.

Ancient Celtic and Indo-European Pagans believed that you were particularly in danger of being attacked by spiteful evil spirits on your wedding day. Of course, no one wants to fend off evil spirits while they're trying to get married, so the Pagans developed a cunning plan. On a bride's wedding day, she would dress her bridesmaids so that they resembled her to the tee. They'd wear the same kind of veil she wore, the same kind of shoes, and an identical dress. The early Pagans thought that seeing multiple identical brides would confuse any evil spirits that may be on the prowl, deterring them from attacking the real bride.

Today bridesmaids are more often tasked with keeping mothers-in-law at bay than they are with fighting off the forces of evil.

Knocking on Wood

Has someone ever said something like, "I've never been in an accident," while in your presence and immediately thereafter said, "knock on wood," before tapping or knocking on the nearest wooden object? This kind of reaction is common all around the world but very few people know why they do it (although so many of us do).

The origin of the "Touch Wood!" phenomenon is, you guessed it, Pagan too. Early Celtic Pagans believed that woodland spirits continued to inhabit wooden objects even after the tree that they had been crafted from had been cut down and made into a doorway or a table. Consequently, they hypothesized that tapping or knocking on a wooden object could wake up any woodland spirits that were living in it, prompting them to offer protection to the speaker or the household in which the dooming words were spoken.

Christmas

Christmas was first celebrated by the Romans about 500-years before the believed date of the birth of Christ. Of course, they didn't call it Christmas. Instead, it was called Saturnalia and it took place on the twenty-fifth of December just like modern Christmas does. However, it wasn't held as a Christian celebration as it normally is today. It was held in honor of the Sun God's victory over the darkness that winter brings. A fitting occasion to celebrate as the Roman winter solstice took place a mere four days before December 25.

Not only did the Romans make use of Saturnalia to celebrate Sol Invictus (the victory of the Sun God), they also used it to celebrate a myriad of lesser Gods' and demigods' birthdays.

Hercules, Mithras, Dionysos, and Adonis were all believed to have been born on this day.

The tradition of giving gifts for Christmas is just as old as Saturnalia is. During Saturnalia, the Pagan Romans would gift their friends and family handmade trinkets (clay figurines were especially popular) at banquets (not unlike modern Christmas dinners) held in honor of Sol Invictus.

Easter

The fact that Easter's date is determined anew every year based off of the Lunar cycle in April is a dead giveaway that it was originally a Pagan holiday. What interest do Christians have in the moon and its phases, after all?

Easter is as old as religion itself is. It likely has its roots in 4,000-year Sumerian beliefs. The Sumerians believed that the Goddess Ishtar traveled down into the underworld in search of her deceased husband, the God Tammuz. During her descent down into the underworld, she's stripped of all of her earthly garbs and is eventually killed and hung from the cavern's roof. One of her assistants immediately noticed that something was wrong, not only was Ishtar missing but the animals on Earth stopped bringing forth offspring, the trees stopped bearing fruit, and all of the crops failed.

After three miserable days on Earth, Ishtar's concerned assistant consulted the other Sumerian Gods for help. Most of them turned the assistant away, but Enki, the water God, heard the assistant's plea and brought forth two strange creatures. He sent the creatures down into the underworld and commanded them to take the tree of life and the water of life with them. They did as they were commanded and soon returned with Ishtar and Tammuz, revived and well.

The Sumerians believed that this revival only lasted for six months, after which Tammuz and Ishtar, who bore the light of the sun, would return to the underworld and toil there for another six months. This constant descent into and ascent from the underworld is how the Sumerians explained the changing of the seasons.

The holiday centered around Ishtar's ascent from the underworld is essentially a celebration of spring. Ishtar herself even borrowed her name to the modern holiday that was inspired by her journey to save her husband: Easter.

New Year's Day

For hundreds of years, the Pagan Romans celebrated the new year in March. March was an important month to the early Romans because it was the month that they dedicated to the worship of Mars, the God who fathered the founder of Rome, Romulus. All of this changed when Julius Caesar introduced the Julian Calendar. The Julian Calendar moved the new year to the first of January, the month that was dedicated to the worship of a god known as Janus. Janus was recognized as being the God of beginnings, which made his month suitable for the Roman new year.

Roman new year celebrations shared some commonalities with modern New Year's Eve celebrations in the sense that the new year was ushered in with a great deal of joyous dancing and feasting. However, there are some noticeable differences too. First, the Romans engaged in ritual animal sacrifice on New Year's Day that involved taking a large white bull up Capitoline Hill and slaughtering it at the top of it in hopes of winning the Gods' favor for the next twelve months. Second, the Roman high priest at the time, known as the Pontifex Maximus, also presented the Gods with a pie (yes, a pie) at the top of the hill as an act of worship.

Halloween

By now, most people are aware of the fact that Halloween was historically known as Samhain (an event that is still prominently featured in the Wiccan Wheel of the Year). The Celtic Pagans first started celebrating Samhain on October 31, thousands of years ago. Although it was technically little more than a harvest festival in practice, the Celts believed that October 31 marked a thinning of the veil between the world of the dead and the world of the living. This "thinning of the veil" meant that spirits and fay were free to spend the day walking among the living.

The Celts were naturally weary that spirit attachments and hauntings could take place on this day and took several measures to protect themselves. They lit large bonfires that they believed were cleansing in the sense that they were believed to chase away any evil spirits that might be lurking nearby, they dressed up in disguises (a tradition that we've kept alive in modernity too) because they thought that the spirits would be unable to follow them home if they did not know their true identities, and they placed turnips with faces carved into them in front of their homes' doorways to frighten off any ghostly evil-doers.

While the Celts were careful not to invite in any evil spirits during Samhain, they welcomed any good spirits (like the souls of deceased relatives) by setting a place at the table for them during dinner and by leaving offerings in the form of apples and nuts outside of their homes for any peckish ghosts who might happen to wander by (not too unlike the bowls of candy that are left out for children during Halloween in modernity).

CHAPTER 3
BELIEFS

It's hard to define exactly what a belief is. Is the knowledge that the sun will come up tomorrow a belief? Is the idea that stealing or murder is wrong a belief? In the religious sense, a belief is an ideological concept that is so supported by the constituents of that religion that it forms an integral part of its theological basis. In this chapter, we'll comb through beliefs that are central to all Pagan belief systems and extrapolate the behaviors which they are meant to encourage and guide.

Like all religions, the various forms of Paganism incorporate a shared set of beliefs that shape the actions, morality, and choices of those who participate in them. It's important to be aware of the fact that Paganism is a very broad religious spectrum, incorporating everything from African ancestor worship to Hinduism. Although some core beliefs are shared across the entire spectrum, many beliefs and practices remain exclusive to a certain belief system or path.

Beliefs That Are Common Among Pagan Religions

While nature-centricity, blessedness, the idea of karma, polytheism, and humanitarianism/humanism are all traits that Pagan religions share, they're not technically shared beliefs. Shared beliefs are far more ideological and abstract. They have been codified in religious texts or are sometimes found in Pagan oral traditions, but their constant presence across the entire Pagan spectrum is notable enough that they've become somewhat synonymous with Paganism itself.

These common beliefs ensure that nearly all forms of Paganism share an identical moral compass or general idea of morality despite otherwise being more varied than any other form of religion. In turn, all Pagans seem to have more or less the same beliefs when it comes to discerning what's right from what's wrong.

Freedom of Choice

While some historical religions or superstitions propagated the idea of fate or destiny, most Pagan religions posit that every individual is responsible for their actions and consequently must bear the consequences of those actions with a fair amount of dignity. Pagan belief systems do not often suggest that any deity or outside force has any control over human thoughts or actions, which means that Pagans can't shirk the eventual outcomes of their decisions by saying, "God works in mysterious ways," or, "Well, it was God's will."

The concept of freedom of choice is further enforced by the fact that most Pagan religions do not threaten their constituents with Heaven or Hell and if they do have separate afterlives for good- and evil-doers. The distinction between the two is usually much more extreme than it is in most mainstream religions (in other words, you won't end up going to 'the bad place' simply for thinking a bad thought, an idea that is prevalent in Abrahamic religions which generally make coveting or jealousy a mortal sin). Freed from the chains of punishment for inconsequential sin, Pagans are freer than others to make decisions based on what they truly feel is right or wrong rather than being told which decision to make by religious scripture.

Connection With the Universe

While many Abrahamic religions (the most popular form of modern religion) posit that their constituents must spend the entirety of their mortal lives seeking a connection with a singular God, Pagans spend the length of their existence connecting with the universe and striving to strengthen and improve that connection.

The ideological concept of "connecting with the universe," is quite broad. It could mean searching for a connection with nature by worshiping nature-centric Gods and Goddesses like Diana or Cernunnos, it could mean striving for enlightenment by cleansing and controlling your energy, it could mean connecting to your fellow human beings through acts of kindness or humanitarianism, or it could mean seeking control over yourself through connecting with the magick of the universe. Regardless of what it means to any particular individual, it represents the will to connect to something bigger than oneself, to a higher energy, and to become one with it rather than to bow down before it.

Personal Responsibility

In chapter one, we discussed the fact that most Pagan belief systems incorporate some concept of Karma or karmic retribution. When you combine the belief that your actions come back to you with the belief in freedom of choice, the inevitable conclusion is the need for, and belief in, personal responsibility.

Pagan belief systems normally incorporate the idea that their constituents are entirely responsible for their actions and must unapologetically bear whatever consequences arise from these, intended and unintended alike. This shared ideology means that it can confidently be asserted that the concept of personal responsibility is central to Paganism itself. Not only do the majority of Pagans believe that every individual is responsible for their actions and choices (largely regardless of the circumstances), they generally also believe that every action or choice committed by an individual comes back to them in some way (this is especially clear when considering the Wiccan "Rule of Three").

While the idea of personal responsibility might seem scary when it's much easier to default back to the concept of "God's will," it is also incredibly empowering once fully embraced. If you're entirely responsible for your actions, you're also entirely responsible for your outcomes which means that you control the direction that your life will take.

The Pagan View of Self

Your "view of self" informs your idea of yourself in relation to the universe. It determines how you treat others, animals, and the natural world. It even influences how you treat yourself. It does this by giving you an idea of where you fit into the world's 'hierarchy.' Do you serve under a higher being? Is that higher being a man or a God/Goddess? Do you believe that committing good deeds helps you to move up this hierarchy? Does this hierarchy place you above animals? Does it place you above other human beings? At the end of the day, our view of ourselves is the singular most influential impression we'll ever have. The Pagan view of self is remarkable and unique in several ways.

Many mainstream religions' view of self is that every human being ever born is a unique being with a singular soul who was created with the sole purpose of worshiping, whatever deity that specific religion propagates, even if it means suffering in the process. This view of self places human beings above animals who do not labor for their specific deity and can lead to a disregard for the natural world as all of its emphasis is placed on the afterlife rather than the current life.

The Pagan view of self raises human beings no higher than the creatures that they share the Earth with and emphasizes the importance of maintaining this world, without being overly concerned or fearful of the next. Pagans see themselves as co-existing with the Gods or Goddesses, and while they're capable of reaching out to them for help and may choose to worship them, they do not consider themselves to be thralls under any particular deity.

Guiding Behaviors

The aforementioned beliefs that are prevalent across the entire spectrum of Paganism naturally give rise to a set of interconnected guiding behaviors. You can't have personal responsibility without having discipline, you won't connect with the universe if you aren't perpetually questioning and searching, and freedom of choice without justice would simply be anarchy.

These guiding behaviors aren't necessarily codified in any Pagan religious texts which means that they aren't officially tenets of Paganism; but that doesn't mean that they aren't universally viewed as desirable by the majority of Pagan belief systems,

It's important to be aware of the fact that this list is not exhaustive. While most Pagan belief systems incorporate each one of the traits mentioned below in some way, shape, or form, different Pagan belief systems may have varying guiding behaviors that may differ quite a lot from each other.

Honesty

Honesty is probably one of the few character traits that seem to be encouraged by every single religion ever conceived of. It makes sense that every ideological system would encourage honesty. In most cases, honesty is the most basic form of kindness. If you do not deceive someone, the chances of you harming them are much lower. Deception isn't only used by serial killers to lure their victims away from crowds, it's used to oppress people (often politically), it's used to incite violence or tension, it's used to misuse laborers and workers, and it's often used to exact control in personal relationships. Very few religions worldwide encourage any of the aforementioned behaviors, so it makes sense that it's simply easier to outlaw the act of lying.

In Paganisms' case, lying isn't just a tool that could be used to hurt someone, it's a weaponization of words. Most Pagans, especially those that believe in Magick, respect the sanctity and power of spoken words. Words that have been uttered can't be taken back and if words have the power to unleash curses and blessings, they certainly have the power to influence the external world when harnessed as a lie. It's important not to influence the external world in unintended ways and thus lying is considered taboo by many Pagan belief systems.

Discipline

The majority of Pagan belief systems out there posit the idea of some kind of karmic retribution. In essence, they believe that if you do bad things, bad things will happen to you. Inversely, the thought is that if you do good things, good things will happen to you. Drawing from this, it seems pretty obvious that most

Pagans would prefer to do 'good things' to receive good things in return. Of course, doing 'good things' all of the time is much more difficult than it sounds. That's where discipline (specifically, self-disciple) comes in.

Ninety-nine percent of Pagan religions encourage their followers to hone their self-discipline to improve the quality of their outcomes. Some attempt to do this by meditating, by chanting mantras, by invoking Gods or Goddesses to improve their resolve, or by calling on guiding spirits. Regardless of how they choose to do it, Pagans are a disciplined bunch who are not only often capable of harnessing all kinds of energies and commanding otherworldly beings, but who are capable of controlling themselves too. The most important control of all.

Justice

Lady Justice was fashioned after a Pagan Roman Goddess named Justitia. Justitia, as her name would suggest, was the Goddess of Justice and was often depicted as being blind-folded while wielding a weighing scale in one of her hands and a sword in the other (an icon that is also often associated with the USA's judicial system).

Lady Justice's Pagan origins mean that it's no surprise that most Pagan religions emphasize the importance of fairness and justness. While it's true that Paganism's definitions of good and evil are much looser than those set by Abrahamic religions, it wouldn't be fair to say that Paganism doesn't encourage the punishment of evil-doers or that Pagan deities aren't ostensibly intent on punishing evil-doers themselves.

The Pagan idea of karmic retribution means that most Pagans believe that evil-doers will be rewarded in this lifetime with as much pain and suffering as they imparted on others. Not only do Pagans believe that evil-doers will get a dose of their own medicine during this lifetime, but they also believe that they alienate themselves from the universe (or whatever cosmic power that specific path subscribes to) by throwing their Karma out of balance, ultimately disconnecting themselves from an afterlife in which they'd become one with the universe (or the aforementioned alternate cosmic power).

The Acceptance of and Co-Existence With Death

Naturally, nobody likes thinking about death (especially not their own). The majority of the mainstream religions out there strive to soften the blow of one's mortality by promising an afterlife that is even better (and more extravagant) than the life that the person had here on Earth. While there's nothing wrong with believing in the Pearly Gates, Paganism tends to take a different approach by positioning death as a natural part of life in the minds of its followers, making it a little easier to accept when it, unfortunately, does become a part of their lives in whatever shape or form.

Not only do many Pagan belief systems believe that you should be as scared of death as you were of your birth (in other words, not at all) but most of them also posit that it's possible for the living to contact the dead through means of magick, rituals, or divination. The fact that the living aren't so far removed from the dead that death means that the deceased is no longer reachable by the living makes death a lot easier to accept because it means that loved ones are no more than a simple spell or ritual away. The idea that the dead can walk among the living as spirits or ghosts is also incredibly prevalent in many Pagan belief systems. This means that the afterlife isn't some great unknown that Pagans feel they need to fear but rather a separate part of the world we currently inhabit.

Questioning and Searching

While prolonged periods of self-doubt are unpleasant at best and reality-shifting at worst, a little self-doubt isn't considered a bad thing if you consider yourself to be a Pagan. Pagans are constantly re-evaluating their beliefs and values to examine them for faults or foibles. This continuous process of self-evaluation means that Pagans regularly offer themselves the opportunity to reflect on their thoughts and actions, and to make improvements where they find faults. It also means that Pagans are generally less prone to simply settling on a singular, unchanging belief system for their entire lives, rather their beliefs and practices change as they change, grow, and become wiser.

It's only human nature to want to become "set in our ways," as a matter of convenience. However, Pagans have to defy this impulse if they truly wish to perfect their practice and achieve that elusive, "connection with the universe," that was discussed earlier.

CHAPTER 4
MAJOR PAGAN PATHS AND THEIR TRADITIONS

There are hundreds of different Pagan paths. Researchers estimate that there are approximately 600 variations in total (and that's when only the ones that are currently still being adhered to are considered). These paths are made distinct by the deities that they worship, their magickal and ritual practices, and their region of origin.

Choosing a Pagan path to embark on can be a little daunting when you consider the sheer number of paths that are up for consideration and how varied all of them are. For this reason, this chapter will only cover the most popular Pagan paths in an attempt to help you to make your selection. If none of the paths that are discussed below resonates with you, you should continue with your search for a suitable belief system by consulting other Pagan texts.

African Diasporic Religions

Africa is often referred to as the cradle of humankind, so it's not surprising that it boasts a host of truly unique Pagan belief systems that are so old that we can't confidently say when people started practicing them. These beliefs were exported to the Americas along with their followers that were so cruelly ripped from their homelands by greedy slave traders. Despite the terrible conditions that many African-Americans' ancestors had to endure, they kept their beliefs and practices alive, even when it meant that they had to practice in secret.

African diasporic religions are the beliefs of the people who were brought from Central Africa hundreds of years ago. However, they no longer exactly resemble the Pagan beliefs that are still practiced in Africa today. Instead, it seems that they were adapted and changed as their followers' circumstances and locations adapted and changed, creating something unique.

African diasporic religions share many common traits like ancestor worship, shamanism, spiritism, a pantheon of divine spirits serving under a single creator deity, and other elements of folk religion.

The most commonly practiced African diasporic religion in the USA is known as Hoodoo. Hoodoo practitioners usually incorporate elements of Christianity into their belief systems too, believing the Abrahamic god to be their creator deity, although they do believe in and call upon lower spirits too.

Alexandrian Wicca

Alexandrian Wicca was developed approximately 60-years ago in Britain by Alex Sanders. The basis of its belief system was crafted from Gardnerian Wicca and was influenced by both Hermetic Qabalah (an esoteric tradition with its roots planted firmly in Jewish religious beliefs) and ceremonial magick.

Alexandrian Wicca is very "loosey-goosey" when it comes to how it expects its followers to conduct their various rituals, rites, and traditions. Unlike other forms of Wicca, it doesn't prescribe the kind of ritual tools (like daggers, altars, or gauntlets) that its followers need to use, instead opting to believe that the practitioners' intentions are more central to a ritual or spell's success than the tools they used are. Alexandrian Wiccans also place less emphasis on the importance of casting spells and working magick, while skyclad (a term that Pagans use to refer to practicing in the nude) which makes it a credible option for introverts who aren't interested in naked dancing but who do want to get involved in some form of Wiccan practice.

Ásatrú

If Odin piques your interest, then Ásatrú might be just the path for you. Ásatrú is essentially a modern revival of the Pagan belief system that the Vikings used to follow. Its modern creation was largely thanks to an Icelandic sheepherder who started collecting ancient religious texts and reworking them in modern contexts in the mid-twentieth century. It was officially recognized in Iceland as a religion, on the same footing as Christianity and Islam, approximately fifty years ago.

Ásatrú is polytheistic which means that its followers worship a great host of ancient Norse Gods and Goddesses. The most important deities on this path are Odin (naturally), Njord, Thor, Freyja, Frigg, Loki, and Freyr.

The most important tenet of Ásatrú is known as the "Nine

Noble Virtues." Adherents of this Pagan belief system spend their entire lives striving to cultivate all nine virtues in their lives. These virtues are perseverance, discipline, courage, self-reliance, truth, fidelity, industriousness, honor, hospitality, and fidelity.

Assianism

If you're interested in embarking on a Pagan path that is nearly 3,000-years old rather than committing to one of the Neo-Pagan belief systems whose religious texts were only written in modernity, then you should consider Assianism.

Assianism is the original belief system that was adhered to by the Scythians. The Scythians were a group of near-legendary Serbian warriors that conquered large parts of the ancient world.

Assianism posits the existence of a single supreme God known as Xwytsau who reveals himself to mankind in several lesser forms of lesser Gods. Those who adhere to this belief system use these lesser Gods as middlemen to communicate with God's supreme form.

This Pagan belief's religious texts state that man is nothing but an even lesser expression of the supreme God, although adherents are keenly aware that this doesn't mean that they're only capable of siding with Xwytsau and that doing evil deeds can quickly align them with Dalimon (evil spirits) instead.

Baltic Neopaganism

Baltic Neopaganism is based on the ancient Pagan beliefs that were held by the Baltic population thousands of years ago. It is a relatively broad term for quite a large movement. The movement consists of two main schools of thought: Romuva and Dievturība.

Romuva is specifically based on the ancient beliefs of Lithuania and has gathered quite a following in its country of origin, seemingly having morphed into a form of patriotism as well as a religion. Romuva is polytheistic, although Zeme (best described as the Earth Goddess or a Mother Earth) and Perkunas (the God of Thunder and Lightning) are recognized as being its most prolific deities.

On the other hand, Dievturība is specifically based on the ancient beliefs of Latvia. Just as is the case in Christianity, adherents of Dievturība believe in a trinity that, when considered as a whole, makes up their supreme being. This trinity is made up of Laima (the God of Fortune and Fire), Māra (the Divine Feminine), and Dievs (the Divine Masculine).

Celtic Wicca

Celtic Wicca is another popular variation of Gardnerian Wicca. Although it has no official date of inception, it seemed to grow in popularity at the turn of the twenty-first century.

The only real difference between Celtic Wicca and Gardnerian Wicca is the fact that Celtic Wiccans have slotted Celtic deities into pre-established Wiccan practices and rituals. The Celts were a group of people who inhabited Central Europe nearly 3,000 years ago. The Celts were driven out of Europe (and exterminated) during the rise of the Republic of Rome.

The main Celtic deities are Lugh (the God of War), Ana (the supreme Goddess), Mórrígan (the Goddess of Destiny), Angus (the God of Love), Dagda (the supreme God), and Brigid (the

Goddess of Health and Healing). These are the deities that are called upon most often by Celtic Wiccans during rituals and spells.

Christian Wicca

Many people mistakenly believe that Christianity and Wicca are opposing religions and thus that combining the two is immoral in some way. I'm here to tell you that there's absolutely nothing wrong with combining these two religious paths if it is the direction that you feel called in.

Christians Wiccans believe that the Abrahamic God is the supreme God. Different variations have different viewpoints when it comes to lesser Gods. Some believe that other Pagan deities (like Celtic or Norse Gods and Goddesses) can be worshiped as lesser Gods without contradicting their Christian beliefs, while others abstain from polytheism and base their entire practice around the Christian God. Neither path is more correct. It's entirely up to each Pagan practitioner how they would ultimately like to conduct their practice.

Most Christian Wiccans do engage in run-of-the-mill Wiccan traditions like magick, divination, and communing with spirits, although some abstain from any preternatural practices that do not involve a blessing or protective magick.

Dianic Wicca

Dianic Wicca is possibly the most unique variation of Gardnerian Wicca. Its adherents ultimately believe that the Feminine Divine is the connection with the universe that they should be seeking and consequently they only worship

Goddesses, shunning the worship of Gods entirely.

Dianic Wiccans often worship a broad spectrum of Goddesses, including members from the Greek, Roman, Norse, and Celtic pantheon, making it an attractive option for Wiccans who are looking to incorporate a subsection of deities from several traditions.

Unfortunately, there are sects of Dianic Wicca that are incredibly exclusionary (even though the traditions which they are based upon emphasize the importance of inclusion). If you are interested in embarking on a Dianic Wiccan path, you're best advised to steer clear of any covens or groups that 'gate keep' their membership in some way.

Druidry

Modern druids have shaped their religious beliefs around what we know about the ancient beliefs of real druids. The original druids lived about 3,000 years ago. They were essentially Celtic priests, although they also acted as judges, lecturers, philosophers, lawmakers, teachers, and healers. All in all, they were pretty important members of Celtic society.

Modern druidism involves the worship of Celtic Gods (much like Celtic Wicca does). Although its true emphasis is placed on living in harmony with the natural world, Druidry also traditionally involves a degree of ancestor worship and the invocation of 'Awen' (the Spirit of the Divine).

Druidry shares a lot of common traits with Wicca. These include the calling of the corners before ceremonies, the use of ritual chalices, gauntlets, or daggers, and the observance of the Wheel of the Year.

Eclectic Paganism (Making Your Own Path)

If there's no single Pagan path that you feel drawn to, you might consider calling yourself an Eclectic Pagan. Eclectic Pagans combine any number of Pagan beliefs, traditions, and rituals into their practice, taking them from any Pagan path that they feel drawn to without feeling obligated to embrace the rest of that path's practices or beliefs.

Eclectic Pagan's beliefs are so varied that any attempt to summarize them would be foiled from the start. While some Eclectic Pagans combine Baltic Neopaganism with Wicca to form the basis of their belief system, others use this term to describe the amalgamation between their sincerely held Christian beliefs and the Norse or Celtic beliefs that they've combined it with.

Faery Faith

Faery Faith is a variation of Dianic Wicca that came into existence approximately 40-years ago. It was inspired by the writings of Margaret Lumley Brown and Mark Roberts, two important members of the modern Neopaganism movement.

Faery Faith's most important tenets are a deeply held respect for nature and the importance (and power) of communing with "the Little Folk." Although you might assume that Faery Faith is based on Celtic Paganism (simply because of the Celts' reverence for faeries), it incorporates beliefs from many different Pagan Paths (it even takes some of its elements from ancient Egyptian Paganism).

Adherents of Faery Faith plan their lives around the "lunar tree energies." These are thirteen distinct energies that they believe accompany the thirteen different Celtic months of the year. Each energy has a different effect, whether it's speeding up personal development or fostering a feeling of jealousy. Followers of this belief system make use of herbal tinctures known as "Bach Flower Remedies" to combat any negative effects that the lunar tree energies might influence over their lives.

Faery Wicca

If you've always felt drawn to elves, woodland spirits, goblins, sprites, or fairies, then Faery Wicca might be the path that you're destined to embark on.

Faery Wicca is another popular variation of Gardnerian Wicca. Its distinguishing feature is the fact that its adherents center their magickal practices and rituals around invoking and honoring some of the natural world's more mischievous entities: the Fae/Fay and creatures that are similar to them.

This Pagan belief system was largely inspired by Kisma Stepanich's literary works. Stepanich theorized that there was a group of people who preceded the Celts who originally brought the concept of magick to the European mainland. Stepanich allegedly identified this population group as "Tuatha De Danaan." Essentially, a group of magickal Irish folk who are believed to have been the human reincarnations of the Celtic Gods.

Gardnerian Wicca

Gardnerian Wicca was the first form of Wicca to be developed in modernity. It was created by Gerald Gardner in the early 1900s. Garner was a retired British public servant when he joined a coven. The fact that he joined a coven isn't nearly as remarkable as the fact that he did it during a time when Britain's Witchcraft Act of 1735 was still in effect. This piece of legislation made it illegal for any British citizen to divine the future, cast spells, or practice any form of magick. Regardless of the inherent danger of joining, the coven that Gardner joined served as the inspiration for the religion which he would create mere years later.

Gardnerian Wiccans are polytheistic, but they worship two main deities: The Horned God (often in the form of Pan or Cernunnos) and the Mother Goddess (often in the form of Freyja or Gaia).

This Pagan path's entire theological basis is centered upon a single "rede." This rede, known as "the Wiccan rede," summarizes the only rule that binds Gardnerian Wiccans into a single sentence: "If it harms none, do as thy wilt."

Hedge Witchcraft

The stereotypical image of a witch who lives in a cottage in the forest and collects herbs to heal the local villagers despite largely being ostracized by them conforms to what would best be described as a Hedge Witch. It's important to note that all practitioners on this path, regardless of their gender or sex, are referred to as Hedge Witches.

Hedge Witches are solitary practitioners which means that they don't belong to any Pagan groups or covens. Their magick is often heavily reliant on herbs and herbology, tools that they use to bring about both physical and mental healing.

Another common trait that many self-identified Hedge Witches claim to share is the fact that they have no formal education in magick or the Pagan beliefs that they embody, rather forming their practice around a "gut feeling" for what feels right.

Due to the non-uniformity of Hedge Witches' beliefs and practices, it can confidently be said that no two are alike. This diversity gives Hedge practitioners the freedom to experiment as they see fit without having to worry about conforming to any set standards or rituals.

Hellenism

Hellenism rose to prominence at the end of the twentieth century. It is a Neopagan religion that incorporates the ancient beliefs and practices of the Greeks with more modern magickal traditions. It has been recognized in Greece as a formal religion, on par with Christianity and Islam, for the past three years.

The term Hellenism was first used about 1,700 years ago by Julian the Philosopher, a prolific Roman Emperor, in reference to the Pagan beliefs of a specific region of Greece at the time.

Hellenists describe their belief system as resting on three pillars of virtue. These pillars are hospitality, virtue, and piety. Hellenists express the virtue of hospitality by being kind and generous towards strangers. This virtue was inspired by the Greek God, Zeus. Zeus is the God of Thunder, but he's equally known for his hospitality towards travelers and foreigners.

Virtue itself is expressed by striving to constantly improve all aspects and areas of one's life, from one's physique to one's business prowess. The modern Hellenists often try to embody this virtue through continuous education, healthy living, and a good dose of ambition.

The Hellenists try to embody the virtue of piety by respecting the ancient Greek Gods, revering them, worshiping them, and living their lives as was prescribed by ancient Greek religious doctrines.

Hellenists are polytheists who lavish most of their worship on twelve main Greek Gods and Goddesses known as "the Twelve Olympians." These twelve Gods are:

- Dionysus (the God of Wine)
- Zeus
- Hermes (the God of Athletes and Thieves)
- Hera (the Goddess of Marriage and Childbirth)
- Aphrodite (the Goddess of Love)

- Poseidon (the God of the Sea)
- Hephaestus (the God of Volcanoes)
- Demeter (the Goddess of Grain and the Harvest)
- Ares (the God of War)
- Athena (the Goddess of War and Wisdom)
- Artemis (the Greek Goddess of Wild Animals and the Hunt)
- Apollo (the God of the Sun and Medicine)

Italo-Roman Neopaganism

Italo-Roman Neopaganism is also often called Roman Polytheistic Reconstructionism and Religio Romana. It saw a surge in popularity in the 1980s that led to a rapid increase in its number of adherents.

Adherents of this Pagan path believe that one must strive to embody two sets of virtues, known as Personal and Public Virtues, to fully embody the Roman way of life and consequently the vision that the Gods have for the mortal world. Both of these sets of virtues are quite expansive, which means that Italo-Roman Neopagans know exactly what they need to strive for to reach their spiritual peak.

The Personal Virtues that Italo-Roman Neopagans believe that they need to strive to embody are:

- Courtesy
- Mercy
- Honesty

- Humanity
- Dutifulness
- Wholesomeness
- Tenacity
- Respectability
- Sternness
- Frugalness

The Private Virtues that they strive to achieve are:

- Courage
- Wealth
- Fertility
- Endurance
- Piety
- Modesty
- Hope
- Providence
- Wealth
- Peace
- Confidence
- Clemency
- Happiness
- Justice
- Liberality

- Equity

Italo-Roman Neopagans are polytheistic but reserve the majority of their worship and reverence for twelve Gods and Goddesses known as "the Council of Twelve." These twelve deities are Vesta, Jupiter, Juno, Ceres, Neptune, Mercury, Minerva, Venus, Vulcan, Diana, Mars, and Apollo.

Kemetism

If you feel drawn to Egyptology, you might be destined to embark on a Kemetic path. Kemetism is a Neopagan path that was founded approximately 50-years ago, in an attempt to revive the belief system that the ancient Egyptians adhered to.

Kemetic Pagans generally adhere to four main traditions: Ancestor worship, the adherence to upholding Ma'at's values (the concepts of truth, justice, equity, and fairness), respect for the community through participation in communal activities, and belief in the supreme being.

Like most Pagans, those who identify as Kemetic are polytheistic. Despite Kemetism's incredibly polytheistic nature (it officially recognizes more than one-hundred Gods and Goddesses), there are a few deities who seem to feature more prevalently. These are Ma'at (the Goddess of Justice), Thoth (the God of Writing), Bast (the Goddess of Cats and Protection), Sekhmet (the Goddess of Healing and War), and Anubis (the God of the Dead).

Mexicayotl

This Pagan path has a pretty tricky name to pronounce (it's pronounced "Mex-ie-kay-ottle") but its core belief system is relatively easy to understand. It was founded exactly 70-years ago in an attempt to revive the ancient Aztecs' religious practices. Naturally, Mexicayotl is most prevalent in South America, although it has gained followers in Africa, Asia, and Oceania too.

Although Mexicayotl recognizes hundreds of Aztec Gods and Goddesses as valid deities, the four most revered entities are Tezcatlipōca (the God of Providence), Huītzilopōchtli (the God of Free Will), Xīpe-Tōtec (the God of Brute Force), and Quetzalcohuātl (the God of Knowledge and Wisdom). These four Gods are single-handedly tasked with ushering in each of the four eras that the Aztecs believed the world would go through before entering the fifth and final era.

Mexicayotl was officially deemed a fully-fledged religion by the Mexican government approximately five years ago and its membership continues to grow exponentially with each passing year. To many Mexicans, Mexicayotl represents a way to reclaim the heritage that was stolen from them by European colonizers.

Odinism

Odinism is one of the older Neopagan movements. It first emerged about 200-years ago and is aimed at observing the religious practices of ancient Germania. This means that it incorporates several different Anglo-Saxon and Norse belief systems, amalgamating them into one indistinguishable religious practice. This mixed-practice is most evident when one considers the range of deities that Odinists worship. These deities are the Norse Gods and Goddesses known as Freyja, Týr, Frigg, Odin, and Thor, and the Anglo-Saxon Gods and Goddesses known as Ēostre, Thunor, and Wōden.

Odinism is distinct from Ásatrú in the sense that it subscribes to a much larger set of beliefs than Ásatrú does. While Ásatrú only honors the beliefs of the Vikings, Odinism reveres all of the beliefs that were held by Germanic tribes for hundreds of years before and after the age of the Vikings.

Rodnovery

Rodnovery is a form of Slavic Paganism that seeks to revive the ancient beliefs held by the populations of Central and Eastern Europe. These beliefs were almost entirely obliterated by the Christianization of the continent which means that it's fortunate that the Slavic people started reclaiming them approximately 200-years ago.

Rodnovery is one of the more conservative types of Paganism. Rodnovers happily and willingly subscribe to traditional gender roles, believing them to be in line with their central belief that the interests of the many are more important than the interests of the few.

Rodnovers believe in a myriad of different Gods. However, they believe that there is a supreme God named Rod and that all other Gods and Goddesses are simply lesser versions or reincarnations of Rod.

Pagans who subscribe to this particular path do not believe that their actions in this world have any effect on the kind of experience that they'll have in the next. Instead, they believe that justice needs to be exacted during a person's mortal life. This belief drives them to seek retribution for any wrongdoing while holding themselves equally accountable for their own mistakes. Rodnovers also generally emphasize the importance of living a 'pure' life, shunning alcohol, tobacco, and many sexual practices in an attempt to achieve this elusive purity or piousness.

While Rodnovery is an honorable path, there are unfortunately some adherents of it who have weaponized it as a way to ostracize anyone who isn't a cis-gendered Caucasian heterosexual. It's important to remember that you can reclaim this path regardless of who you are, who you love, or what you look like despite some malevolent people seeking to twist its truth for their benefit.

Stregheria

Stregheria is a form of traditional Italian witchcraft with a dash of Wicca, neatly bundled into a Neopagan package. It is similar to Wicca as it shares a fair number of magickal rituals with it, its adherents observe the Wheel of the Year, and its rituals often involve the use of daggers, gauntlets, altars, and chalices. It's also similar to Wicca in the sense that most of its deity-worship is centered around the Mother Goddess (Tana) and the Horned God (Tanus) despite it otherwise recognizing a whole host of divine entities too. Regardless of these similarities, its adherents claim that they're nothing but a coincidence, stating that Stregheria is made up of several magickal practices that have been passed down in families throughout the generations and that it drew no, or very little, inspiration from Gardnerian Wicca.

Stregheria encourages its adherents to conduct their rituals and magick, while skyclad (in the nude) and also heavily incorporates elements of divination, ancestor worship, and herbology.

CHAPTER 5
DEITIES

The previous chapter only revealed the tip of the iceberg when it comes to the incredible variety and diversity of the Pagan paths out there. There are hundreds of different Pagan paths and each has its own variations and sects. With such an unbelievable amount of Pagan belief systems currently in existence, it's no surprise that there are thousands of Pagan Gods who are still being worshiped in modernity.

Committing the name of every Pagan God out there to memory would be an insurmountable task. For this reason, this chapter only discusses the most prevalent and widely worshiped deities around the globe.

Most Commonly Worshiped Pagan Deities

You'll undoubtedly encounter Gods and Goddesses that resonate with you more than others do on your journey down a

Pagan path. Some practitioners feel so drawn to a specific God or Gods that they shun all other deities to focus all of their energy on the worship of that specific deity (or deities). Finding a God or Goddess that you feel that you're able to commune with and understand can take a fair bit of searching, so don't be too disheartened if none of the deities on this list seem to draw you in, you might just need to familiarize yourself with some more divine entities.

Aphrodite

When it comes to interesting beginnings, the Greek Goddess of Love, Aphrodite, probably had the most interesting of all. Ancient Greek mythology tells us that Uranus, the God of the Sky, had his genitals cut off by his obviously-rather-angry son, Cronus. In his rage, Cronus tossed Uranus's severed member into the ocean. The amputated body part had scarcely touched the water when it began to foam, the sea's apparent reaction to coming into such a strange form of contact with divinity. Legend has it that Aphrodite was born from this foamy mess.

The ancient Greeks believed that Aphrodite had two consorts who traveled with her wherever she went. They were said to be two male Gods called Dionysus and Ares. Dionysus was worshiped as the God of Wine and Festivities while Dionysus was honored as the God of War. Their more masculine and brash attributes were said to compliment Aphrodite's more feminine and sensual ways. She had seven children with Ares and another six with Dionysus, even though she was believed to have been married to the God of Metalwork, Hephaestus.

As one of the twelve Olympians, Aphrodite is historically quite an important figure across the entire spectrum of Pagan religion. She was worshiped by the ancient Greeks and still is by a great number of Wiccan and Hellenistic practitioners. She even has an entire Neopagan religion based on nothing but her sole worship and veneration called the Church of Aphrodite.

Apollo

These days Apollo's name is often associated with the National Aeronautics and Space Administration's (NASA) famous spacecraft but thousands of years ago he was synonymous with the arts, healing, prophecy, and the sun. Just like Aphrodite, Apollo is one of the Gods that make up a group of all-powerful deities known as the Twelve Olympians. His family tree assured that the Greeks respected him from the start. Greek myths claim that he was sired by no other than Zeus himself, arguably Ancient Greece's most powerful deity.

Unfortunately, his mother, Leto, wasn't nearly as well-respected, especially not by Zeus's wife, Hera, who was furious to learn of Leto's pregnancy and forbade her from giving birth on Earth among mortal men. Leto's banishment forced her to give birth on a floating, ethereal island. Legend has it that Apollo was born wielding a sword made out of pure God (his poor mother) and immediately demanded to be handed a lyre after exiting the birth canal, playing it perfectly by the time he was a couple of days old. Not only was his dad the most feared God on the block, but he was fortunate enough to be born alongside a very influential twin, Artemis (the Goddess of the Hunt).

Zeus's wife never forgave Leto for seducing her husband and sent mythical creature after mythical creature to assault her, starting with an enormous serpent and a giant named Tityos. Apollo didn't take lightly to the attacks on his mother and committed his first two acts of heroism by using the golden sword that he had been born grasping to slay both creatures. The God of the Sun spent quite a large portion of his youth battling a whole host of beings to please his mother, even going as far as slaughtering the seven sons of a Goddess who had mocked Leto's abilities as a mother.

One of Apollo's most remarkable qualities is the fact that Greek mythology openly and proudly describes him as having been bisexual. He had many female lovers, including two nymphs named Daphne and Evadne, and just as many male lovers, including a Spartan prince named Hyacinth.

In modernity, Apollo is still worshiped by Pagans on a variety of different paths. He's especially popular among Gardnerian Wiccans, Hellenists, and other ancient Greek polytheistic revivalists.

Ares

While Apollo has the misfortune of being born as a result of one of Zeus's extra-marital affairs (and spent his life fighting monsters because of it), Ares was lucky enough to have been born as one of Zeus's legitimate sons out of his marriage with Hera. While his legitimacy certainly made his childhood easier, he grew into a brute of a God, seeking violence and conflict wherever he could and thus earning himself the title of 'God of War.' His bloodlust was so insatiable that his father, Zeus, admitted to hating him for it.

He spent his days looking for a fight while driving around in his flaming chariot along with his romantic partner, Enyo (a lesser Goddess of War), and his two sons, Deimos (the God of Terror) and Phobos (the God of Fear who lends his name to fear-disorders in the form of the word 'Phobia').

As he matured, he spent more and more time with Aphrodite, often acting as her consort. Their relationship soon turned romantic, forcing them to sneak around behind Aphrodite's husband's back. Ares soon recruited Alectryon, a dashing young soldier, to watch the door while he was 'visiting' Aphrodite and to warn them if he heard Aphrodite's husband coming. On one fateful morning, Alectryon dozed off in front of Aphrodite's chamber-door. He slept so deeply and so soundly that he never heard Aphrodite's husband approaching. As you can imagine, Aphrodite's husband was furious at what he discovered, setting a trap made out of a net of gold to ensnare the lovers should they ever commune again. Ares was rather upset too and promptly turned Alectryon into a rooster to punish him for snoozing while on duty.

Just like most of the Gods and Goddesses that belong to the Greek pantheon, Ares is still revered by the Hellenists. He is also sometimes called upon or invoked by Wiccan and Druid magick practitioners to aid them in their craft.

Artemis

If you're into strong, powerful female characters, you're going to love Artemis. As mentioned earlier, Artemis is Apollo's twin sister. Unlike Apollo, she was much less prone to fighting monsters and seemed to enjoy healing women and protecting young girls much more. Artemis had such a propensity for helping women out that she was said to have acted as her mother's midwife while her twin brother was being born mere moments after she came into this world.

It is said that Artemis grew into a beautiful woman who spent much of her time practicing her archery with her golden bow and arrows in the mountains. Her beauty made men and Gods alike lust after her, but she wasn't nearly as interested in them as they were in her, instead choosing to spend her time alone. She didn't take kindly to men who tried to force themselves on her either. Greek mythology tells us that she smote a son of Uranus for even just daring to think about raping her, turned a Peeping Tom named Siproites into a young girl for hiding in a nearby berry bush to watch her bathe in a local river, and turned Actaeon, her hunting companion, into a stag for trying to sexually assault her. Being turned into a stag might not sound that bad, but she then promptly sent her hunting hounds to tear him limb from limb.

Artemis has become somewhat of a feminist symbol, so it's easy to understand why her following has increased tenfold in recent years too. She's one of the central deities in the Dianic Wiccan belief system and plays a smaller (although no less significant) role in many Wiccan, Druid, and other Neopagan spiritual practices.

Cerridwen

You might not feel drawn to any of the Gods in the Greek pantheon and that's okay too. Luckily, deities like Cerridwen exist that allow Pagan practitioners to add a Celtic flavor to their spiritual practices.

Cerridwen is also known as the "Keeper of the Cauldron." A nickname that she naturally earned for her ability to brew just about any potion man could imagine. Her command of her cauldron also earned her the title "Goddess of Wisdom."

Celtic lore tells us that she only ever stepped away from her cauldron to give birth to her two children, a daughter named Crearwy and a son named Afagddu. Cerridwen loved both of her children dearly but the rest of the Welsh villagers who lived nearby didn't agree. Crearwy was everyone's favorite. She was not only unbelievably beautiful, but she was also unimaginably kind. Afagddu, on the other hand, was said to have been repulsive in appearance with an even uglier heart. Cerridwen knew that Crearwy would have an amazing life regardless of where she went because of her good looks and her charming personality, she was more concerned about what would become of Afagddu.

This concern drove her to devise a cunning plan: She would concoct a potion that would give Afagddu knowledge of all things, an ability that would certainly improve his standing in the eyes of the Welsh villagers who lived nearby. Unfortunately, her plan was foiled by a clumsy peasant boy whom she had hired to stir the cauldron in which this potion was brewing for exactly one year and one day. Although Afagddu never received the potion that was supposed to make him likable, Cerridwen is still remembered as a Goddess who was capable of near-impossible magickal feats and a prolific enchantress. Due to this, many modern Pagan still call on her when they're casting spells or trying to communicate with the spirit world.

Those who feel drawn to ancient Celtic mythology might want to consider incorporating her into their list of revered deities as she has been renowned for lending a helping hand to her adherents since her worship first began hundreds, if not thousands, of years ago.

Cernunnos

Cernunnos is your archetypal "horned God" which means that he's an incredibly important figure to many Wiccans who lavish a great deal of their worship onto him (or onto Pan in his place in certain cases). Just like Cerridwen, Cernunnos is a Celtic God who was first worshiped in Britain and its surrounding isles hundreds of years ago.

As a Horned God, Cernunnos is tasked with caring for and ruling over wild animals and the fruits of the forest. Even though the first depiction of him has been carbon-dated to be approximately 1,900 years old, there are very few written accounts that make mention of him. This is likely because most Gaelic and Celtic traditions were not recorded in writing during the time that his worship was most prevalent. The little we do know about Cernunnos points to the probability that he was a central figure in Celtic fertility rituals and was likely seen as an embodiment of masculine energy itself.

Although we don't know nearly as much as we'd like to about Cernunnos, that hasn't stopped Neopagans from adopting their own tales about him and making him an important element of their modern spiritual practices. Most Wiccan practitioners believe that he is largely responsible for the seasons (alongside the Mother Goddess). They believe that winter is brought on by his death and that the warmer months only arrive again due to his yearly resurrection. He has also been embraced as a central deity by many druids and eclectic Pagans.

Diana

Diana was one of the Roman Deities that formed the Council of Twelve. Much like the Greek Artemis, she was worshiped as the Goddess of the Hunt and Childbirth. Interestingly, Diana has an awful lot in common with Artemis, more than just her official divine title. She was also believed to have a twin brother named Apollo and although the Romans believed that her mother was named Latona, the rest of her birth story resembles that of Artemis to the tee. Not only is Diana recognized as one of the most powerful Roman Gods, but she is also one of the oldest having come into existence before Rome itself was founded approximately 1,500-years ago.

Diana is said to be a virgin Goddess, shunning the advances of other Gods and Goddesses alike, choosing to spend her time prowling through the countryside with her pack of hunting dogs.

Much like the Celts, the Romans speculated that the seasons occurred because of the annual death and resurrection of a deity. However, unlike the Celts, the Romans believed that this 'deity' was the King of Nemi instead of Cernunnos. Diana's main role was believed to be helping the King of Nemi to return to life to harrow in the spring after every winter, making her somewhat of a recognized healer too. The Romans also speculated that she might be responsible for the lunar phases, often involving her in lunar rituals and traditions.

Diana remains one of the most widely worshiped deities in modern Neopagan communities. She is revered by Wiccans, Roman Neopagans, and Stregheria practitioners alike. She is often honored as representing the Feminine Divine and has consequently inspired a host of feminist Pagan movements. Dianic Wicca, which unfortunately can't be said to subscribe to intersectional feminism in many cases, is entirely built upon her teachings and her worship.

Eros

Eros is Aphrodite's son, so it's no surprise that he turned out to be the God of Lust. His name means "desire" in ancient Greek. Eros was incredibly loved by the ancient Greeks, with hordes of cults dedicated to his worship and his worship alone popping up everywhere during the pre-Classical era. Temples were erected in his honor, dashing statues were carved to resemble him, and sacrifices were made in his honor on the fourth day of every month.

Modern-day cupid was largely inspired by this God (although I'm sure that Eros would be slightly offended to see the chubby baby depictions of him that are most prevalent around Valentine's Day). He was said to own a bow that shot arrows made out of gold that caused whoever they struck to fall in love with the first person they saw, but he was also said to own arrows that made out of lead that had the opposite effect, causing anyone who was hit by one to develop a passionate hate for the first person they saw thereafter.

Eros didn't just make women fall in love with men, though. Even back then he realized that love was love. He was so intent on supporting homosexual relationships that he teamed up with Hermes, the Herald of the Gods, and Heracles, a legendary warrior, to bless all homosexual men with loyalty, physical beauty, eloquence, and strength.

In modernity, Eros is still called upon during some Wiccan binding and fertility rituals and is also worshiped by Roman Neopagans and adherents of Stregheria alike.

Freya/Freyja

The Roman and Greek Gods and Goddesses all have incredibly colorful and often inspiring backstories, but many Pagan practitioners swear that they feel more attracted to Scandinavian and Germanic deities. If you're one of those practitioners, you'll need to familiarize yourself with Freyja (often also spelled 'Freya') to perfect your spiritual practice.

Freyja is a pretty colorful character herself. Norse mythology describes her as traveling from place to place in a flying golden chariot that is pulled by two black cats. She is also known to take her best friend, a boar (yes, a boar) named Hildisvíni, with her on these epic chariot rides across the sky. She also rules over a place called Fólkvangr. Norse mythology describes Fólkvangr as a divine field that receives and hosts the souls of warriors who have died in battle.

When she's not welcoming the immortal souls of fallen warriors or spending time with Hildisvíni, she wanders around on Earth searching for her ever-absent husband called Óðr (a God who is known for nothing other than being Freyja's husband which should give you a clear idea of just how amazing she is). Legend says that all of the red-gold found on Earth came from solidified tears that Freyja shed while mournfully looking for her spouse.

In antiquity as well as modernity, Freyja is honored as being the Goddess of Love, Sex, Gold, Beauty, Fertility, and War. That's a sizable domain for a single deity to rule over. Norse Neopagans and certain groups of Ásatrú practitioners still call upon her when conducting marriage and fertility ceremonies.

Frigga

You might know Frigga as she was portrayed by Rene Russo in the Marvel Cinematic Universe's movies. In ancient Norse mythology, she was the Goddess of the Earth and was believed to be the one and only spouse of Odin. While Odin is fondly known as the "All-Father," few people know that Frigga was originally worshiped as the "All-Mother," a term she deserved after going through the trauma of raising Loki as her stepchild, a kindness that he rewarded for by killing one of her biological sons, Baldur.

Frigga learned that Loki was planning to murder Baldur months before his death and immediately flew into action to concoct a clever plan that would help her to save her beloved son. She decided to make a pact with every animal, plant, stone, river, and tree on Earth, offering them good fortune if they promised in return never to harm Baldur, no matter the circumstances.

They all eagerly agreed, welcoming the idea of her Godly protection. However, Frigga never met with the lowly mistletoe, completely forgetting about it in her consultation with the other material objects. Loki, being the cunning trickster that he is, followed Frigga and noticed that she forgot to ask the same favor of mistletoe. He fashioned a dart out of this festive shrub and used it to assassinate Baldur. Norse mythology suggests that Frigga was never the same again after her son's untimely passing.

In modernity, Frigga is worshiped by a whole range of Norse Neopagans and has also gathered enough Wiccan adherents that her role in their spiritual practices is also worth mentioning.

Mars

Mars was the ancient Roman's God of War. He was widely worshiped and often incorporated in military traditions because of the protection which he was believed to grant soldiers during battle.

Legend says that Mars was born to Juno, the Goddess of Marriage and Fertility. However, unlike most Roman or Greek deities, he isn't reported as having a divine or mortal father. Instead, Mars' adherents believe that Juno conceived him by impregnating herself with a magical flower that granted the gift of fertility to anything that it touched.

Myth says that Mars married the Goddess of War, Nerio. Together this powerful pair decided the outcome of many wars and ruled over the lives of warriors. However, it wouldn't be fair to say that the Romans only ever called on Mars for assistance with violent military clashes, they also prayed to him to protect their crops and to keep rust at bay. The Romans regularly sacrificed bulls, rams, and boars to him, and once a year, in October, they'd even slaughter a horse (an incredibly valuable animal during the height of Mars's worship) in his honor.

In modernity. Mars is still revered by Roman Neopagans and Stregheria practitioners although several Wiccan sects have also been known to invoke him for magickal assistance and blessings.

Morrighan

If you were an Irishman running into battle two-thousand-years ago and you suddenly saw a dark silhouette on the horizon known as The Morrighan or simply 'Morrighan.' Morrighan is an ancient Irish goddess who was believed to be the spouse of the supreme God, Dagda. She was a powerful deity and a feared sorceress in her own right and had a habit of making an appearance before or during important battles to give prophecies on their outcomes. When the battle was over, she'd appear as a murder of crows to peck away at the flesh of the dead.

The ancient Irish Pagans believed that their Gods came to Ireland when a tribe known as Tuatha Dé Danann arrived at its shores and made themselves home. Morrighan was believed to have come to Ireland along with the first Tuatha Dé Danann settlers.

Morrighan is no less revered in modern times. She still has quite an impressive Celtic Neopagan following and is sometimes worshiped alongside Diana by certain sects of Dianic Wiccans.

Odin

Most people know Odin's name even though most of his adherents lived approximately two-thousand years ago. Thanks to the Marvel Cinematic Universe, a lot of people are familiar with his one-eyed, long-bearded visage too. Odin is best known as "the Allfather." Not much is known about how Odin was born or his childhood but historians have been able to surmise what his lineage was. Ancient Norse mythology tells us that Odin was the son of two giants who themselves were descendants of the vicious frost giants who had ruled over the Earth before the time of men.

One of Odin's most unique features is the fact that he is one of the few deities known to mankind whose own prophecy predicts his demise. His adherents believe that his life will be ended during Ragnarök, the end of the world. Until then, he's believed to wander through the world of mortal men, often offering assistance to travelers and divine insights to those who will listen.

Odin is still revered as the primary deity of most Norse Neopagan practitioners and is also central to the beliefs of Ásatrú adherents all around the world.

Thor

Thor is Odin's most famous and most beloved son. Considering that Odin was born of two giants and Thor's mother, Hlödyn, was a giant too, it's entirely reasonable to say that Thor himself was also a direct descendant of the feared frost giants with no dilution to the fierce, frosty blood that ran through his veins. While there's nothing wrong with being a giant, it's pretty odd that Thor was one by birth because he spent much of his time hunting them. His most famous conquest over them occurred after he slew the great giant, Hrungnir, for boasting that he could single-handedly topple Asgard.

Thor didn't just go after boastful giants either, he spent much of his time wandering the icy wastelands that they inhabited looking for any members of the species that he could pick off.

In Norse mythology, it seems as though the giants were seen as something to be exterminated because they threatened the stability of Midgard, the world of men. If that's the case, we should all be pretty thankful that Thor has kept them at bay all of these years.

Just as is the case with his father, little is known about Thor's upbringing and youth. Most accounts of his life seem to recall a time that he was already fully grown. Luckily, the bounty of information that we have about his life as an adult makes up for the scarcity of accounts about his earlier years. We know that Thor married a beautiful fertility Goddess known as Sif (and also that his betrothal didn't stop him from seeking out other lovers, some mortal, some divine, and some giant in size).

Thor's hammer, Mjölnir, is central to his identity. It's the symbol that is most often associated with him and was a major source of power that served to aid him in numerous battles. Thor had been gifted Mjölnir, a hammer that could control lightning and that couldn't be lifted by anyone other than Thor himself, by his brother, Loki. Loki had cut off a lock of Sif's mesmerizing hair in an attempt to prank his brother. Thor did not see the humor in the situation and scolded Loki for being so inconsiderate. Loki felt uncharacteristically ashamed of his actions and traveled to the world of Dwarves to ask for their aid in begging Thor's forgiveness. They lent him the helping hand that he needed in the form of several master-crafted items made out of steel, iron, and gold. Among these gifts was a new head of hair made out of gold for Sif and a fearsome hammer (Mjölnir) for Thor.

Thor is still regularly worshiped as a deity by Norse Neopagans and Ásatrú practitioners alike.

Venus

A lot of Pagan paths that are centered on Goddess worship revere Venus as one of their main deities. Venus is a rather likable deity in every way imaginable, so it's not hard to imagine why her worship has remained popular despite her last temple having been abandoned about 1,000 years ago. Even back in ancient times, Venus was such a popular figure that Julius Caesar tried to claim that he was one of her direct descendants.

Venus was originally honored as the Roman Goddess of Beauty and Love, and also took it upon herself to personally act as the divine guardian of sex workers lovers. Like many other Roman Gods and Goddesses, she embraced all kinds of love. Roman Pagan Mythology tells us that she took just as many women as lovers as she did men, enjoying the company of both equally.

Remarkably, Venus even fell in love with a mortal man named Adonis. Adonis was known all around the world for his unmatched physical beauty (an attribute that I'm sure wasn't lost on Venus). She so loved him that she spent several years on

Earth living in a homely house near the edge of the woods with him. She often warned Adonis that she couldn't offer him protection wherever he went and that not all earthly creatures would treat him kindly just because he was beautiful. Unfortunately, he didn't heed her morning and tragically got mauled to death by a wild boar while out hunting. Venus was the first person to come across the bloody scene. She immediately slumped to the floor and wept for her true love, scooping up his blood in her hands and allowing it to mix with her tears. The Romans believed that this amalgamation fell to the floor and became the first red anemone flower.

How to Engage a Deity

Most mainstream religions place their deities on a pedestal where they're inaccessible to mortal men through any means other than prayer. This is not the case in most, if not all, Pagan paths. The majority of Pagans believe that you can summon or 'evoke' Gods or Goddesses to ask them for advice or to request their assistance in some kind of earthly affair.

Although each Pagan belief system has its own traditions and rituals when it comes to communing with its Gods and Goddesses, they all seem to follow more or less the same process to do so. Traditionally, there are two ways to involve a divine being in a magickal ceremony, through invocation or evocation.

Evocation is the simpler of the two options. When you 'evoke' a deity, you're essentially calling upon it and asking it to lend you its ear or to join you in spirit while you conduct a ritual or spell. An evocation can be as straightforward as saying, "Please bless us with your presence," to whichever God or Goddess you'd like to involve in your workings. You don't need any specialized tools, fellow Pagans, or lengthy rituals to master the art of evocation (although it is said to take a fair bit of luck and practice to do so).

Invocation is the trickiest choice when it comes to communing with the Gods and Goddesses. When you invoke a deity, you're asking it to possess you (albeit, usually only temporarily). The problem with invoking a deity is that you lose control of your physical body and agency while you're possessed by it, which means that you have to be sure that the entity that you've made contact with is the God or Goddess that you intend on communing with before concluding the ceremony. Several different invocation ceremonies have become popular in modernity among Neopagans, the most popular of these is known as "Drawing Down the Moon." "Drawing Down the Moon," is Wiccan in origin but has since been adopted and adapted by many Neopagan paths.

In its most basic form, a Drawing Down the Moon ceremony can be performed by a lone practitioner without having to make use of any props, religious icons, symbols, or tools. All you'd need to carry it out is to create a north-facing altar (a small table laden with trinkets representing the God or Goddess you'd like to invoke and containing small offerings like food or drink that you'd like to make to the deity). Once your altar is all set up, you'd need to wait for the sun to set on the first night of a new moon.

When darkness has fallen, you'd need to stand in front of the altar with your arms extended to the sky and your feet spread a shoulder's width apart. At this point, you'd start with your invocation chant. This chant's format and content will depend on the entity that you're trying to invoke. Although several pre-written chants are available, there's no shame in creating your own (in fact, self-written chants are often reported to be more effective). An invocation chant might look a little like this, "I call upon you Thor, God of Thunder and Lightning, hear my plea and take possession of my mortal body so that I may do your bidding." You'd repeat your chosen invocation chant over and over again until you start feeling the deity's presence.

Many Pagan belief systems discourage their adherents from attempting an invocation until they're very familiar with the God or Goddess who they plan on invoking. Thus, it's not something that you should enter into lightly.

Pagan Views on the Devil and Angels

The devil is a very Pagan concept. It's no mere coincidence that depictions of the Christian devil so closely resemble those of Pagan horned Gods like Pan and Cernunnos, some historians even believe that they're one and the same being, with the same foundational mythology. Although Pan is very different from Lucifer, one can't help but agree that their cloven-hoofed appearances are eerily similar (although the jury is still out on whether they're essentially the same deity).

Despite the similarities in their appearances, Pagans don't believe in "the devil" in the same way that many other religious people do. Very few Pagan deities are entirely good or entirely evil which makes it very difficult to single out an individual one to lay all the blame for the world's ills on. Instead of shying away from their horned Gods, Pagans embrace them in their totality.

Most horned Gods are believed to be fertility Gods. On top of that, they often act as consorts (divine assistants) to the supreme Goddess of the Pagan path that they belong to, aiding her in her quests and supporting her vision for the world. The concept of divine entities being either entirely good or entirely bad, with no middle ground to be found in between, seems to be a largely Abrahamic tradition that doesn't seem to have made its way into any significant Neopagan movements.

Angels are an entirely different kettle of fish. There doesn't seem to be any major consensus within the Pagan community on whether they exist or not, with little agreement on the subject being reached even within well-established Pagan paths with well-documented beliefs. Every practitioner must decide for themselves whether or not they believe that angels are real and whether or not they believe that angels can be contacted through magickal ceremonies like invocations.

It's worth mentioning that many different belief systems posit the existence of angels. They're mentioned in the Bible, the Torah, and the Bible, and many esoteric forms of spirituality also strongly support the idea of their existence. From a Pagan point of view, it makes sense that they might exist. Traditionally, angels have been messengers of God, so it's entirely plausible that messengers of Pagan Gods and Goddesses could also be referred to as angels.

It's important to be conscious of the fact that most Pagan religions predate the concept of the devil and angels. This means that you'll need to adapt any path that you choose to follow to include them should you wish to incorporate them into your belief system.

Is Paganism Compatible With Christianity?

A lot of people feel drawn to Paganism but are concerned that it contradicts their sincerely held Christian beliefs. It's easy to understand why some Christians would shy away from Paganism.

The Bible is full of verses like Leviticus 19:31 that forbids Christians from consorting with spirits; Leviticus 20:27 that condemns spiritual mediums to death, Revelation 21:8 that prophesied that those who practice witchcraft will burn in hell during the end times, Galatians 5:19-20 that describes magick as a "sin of the flesh," and Deuteronomy 18:10-14 that suggests the death penalty for those that practice magick, talk to spirits, or predict the future.

Despite the fact that all of this might seem a little damning, the growing Christian Pagan population believes that these verses were aimed at practitioners of magick and mediums who were using their abilities for nefarious purposes, arguing that these rules were aimed at condemning black magick but not necessarily all other kinds of magick. It's a sound argument and one that's definitely worth some consideration, especially when you take into account that many modern Pagans use their magickal abilities or connection with the spirit world to heal and help people, aid that certainly shouldn't be condemned just because it's a little unconventional.

Other Christian Pagans are resolute in their decision to follow the Bible to the tee but identify as Pagan nonetheless, avoiding any moral pitfalls by simply avoiding any magickal practices or communion with spirits that might be forbidden by the applicable bible verses. It's certainly possible to be Pagan and to live your life in such a way that it mirrors the values of Paganism without ever engaging in any form of magick or making contact with any spirits or entities.

CHAPTER 6
MAGIC(K)

Magick is the most intriguing facet of many Pagan belief systems. I mean, who doesn't want to learn how to bend reality to their will? We'd all like to feel a little more in control of the external world at times so it's no surprise that learning how to do so is what draws so many people to Paganism as a spiritual path.

As mentioned previously, you'll notice that Pagan magick is referred to as 'magic' with a 'k.' This is done to differentiate it from stage magic and slide of hand, the kind of tricks that you're likely to see on stage. Pagan magick normally isn't nearly as flashy, aiming for long-term results rather than the production of short-term illusions.

Different Types of Magick

There are hundreds of different types of Pagan magick because there are hundreds of different Pagan paths populated by hundreds of thousands of individual practitioners, each of who have likely personalized their beliefs and magickal practices in some way. Paganism is about having the freedom to carve out your own spiritual path after all.

Despite this unimaginable diversity, there are still certain 'types' of magick that are more popular than others. It's worth familiarizing yourself with some of the more commonly practiced forms to give yourself a better idea of the kind of magick you would like to dabble in.

Animal Magick

Animal magick is the fluffiest kind of magick. If you feel particularly drawn to our four-legged brethren, you might want to consider centering your magickal practices on it. Practitioners of this kind of magic employ the help of willing animals to help them to work their spells and to complete their rituals. They do so either by lending their energy to the Pagan who they're serving to improve their magickal prowess or by playing a role in a magickal ceremony by allowing themselves to be used as a temporary vessel for a deity or other higher being.

The most important facet of animal magick is consent. It simply doesn't work if the animal who you're involving isn't a willing participant. This means that you might have to spend some time building up a repertoire with the creature you're planning on using as an accomplice in your magickal practices before you're actually able to do so.

Astral Magick (And Astral Travel)

To understand astral magick, you first have to understand the astral plane. The astral plane is sometimes referred to as "the Inbetween." It's often called this because it is believed to be the world that exists in between the world of the living and the world of the dead. It's not entirely material in nature but neither is it ethereal like the spirit world is said to be. Some practitioners believe that it is home to the Fay, others believe that it hosts angels. Regardless of what lives there, magick practitioners worldwide agree that it's a place of immense power that can be used to tap into the spirit world and to materially change the world of the living.

Astral magick refers to magick practices, spells, rituals, blessings, or bindings that are performed while the practitioner is in the astral plane. Magick that is performed while the practitioner is in the astral plane is said to be far more powerful and effective than magick that is performed in the world of the living. The tricky part is learning how to access the astral plane.

The simplest way to do so is through astral projection or astral travel. Both of these terms refer to a phenomenon in which a magick practitioner has trained themselves to allow their spirit to temporarily leave their body. Astral travel gives you instant access to the astral plane. Learning how to do so can take a bit of practice, though. Many prolific Pagans claim that the easiest way to learn to do it is through prolonged meditation, while others claim that it's easiest to do when you're lucid dreaming. Either way, it's not a type of magick that you should dabble in lightly nor is it one that will be accessible to you at the very beginning of your Pagan journey because of the considerable amount of practice and discipline that it requires.

Blood Magick

Almost every culture that has ever existed has recognized the unique power of blood. It makes sense that human beings would be fascinated by blood, we're made out of the stuff after all. Most blood magick practitioners believe that blood can be used to enhance their spells, divination, or other rituals because of the special "life force" that it contains.

Blood can be incorporated into Pagan magick in several ways; it can be mixed into potions, used to draw sigils or runes, consumed before an invocation, or smeared over divination tools. Whichever way it's incorporated, it's believed to amplify the practitioner's natural magickal abilities.

The problem with blood magick is that human blood can be hard to come by. Animal blood is reportedly entirely ineffective. Most practitioners opt to prick their own finger to get a drop or two, some braver practitioners have even been known to use menstrual blood.

If you do choose to make use of blood magick, it's important to avoid any moral quandaries or health risks by only using your own blood and only using a droplet or two at a time.

Crystal Magick

Crystal healing has become incredibly popular in recent years but few people are aware of its Pagan origins. The ancient Egyptians were the first group of people who left records for modern archaeologists to find detailing how they used a variety of different crystals to treat a myriad of ailments and injuries. Today, celebrities like Gwyneth Paltrow swear by their effectiveness too.

Crystal magick can be used for far more than just healing. They're often incorporated in divination rituals and spell work. Many crystal magick practitioners wear them for spiritual and physical protection too.

Every crystal has a unique set of abilities and uses. Crystals also need to be cared for in a certain way and have to regularly be cleansed to remain effective Consequently, you'll need to devote some time familiarizing yourself with them and their care if you're hoping to incorporate them into your magickal practices.

Elemental Magick

Certain people swear that they feel drawn to one of the elements more than all of the others, claiming that their magick is most effective when they incorporate that specific element into the ritual. If you feel particularly drawn to the element of water, your magickal abilities might be amplified if you perform your rituals near a lake, a river, or the ocean. If you feel drawn to fire, you might want to consider lighting some candles before diving into any spell work.

If you believe in astrology, you might consider looking to it for guidance regarding which element would suit you best. All star signs are either air, water, fire, or earth signs. This classification is said to be indicative of the element that will most resonate with you.

Elemental magick is one of the easier forms of magick to get involved in which makes it a fantastic choice for beginner Pagans.

Energy Magick (and Energy Work)

All matter is simply an expression of energy. If you can control energy, you can control matter, and if you can control matter, you can change just about anything you like about the spirit world.

In recent years, energy magick has often been toned down and called "energy work" to make it marketable to the masses. Practices like Reiki, acupuncture, and reflexology all fall under the umbrella term of "energy work." While it's undoubtedly fantastic that energy magick is so often being used to help people and to treat any number of spiritual and physical ailments, it can be used for so much more than just that.

Pagans who make use of energy magick believe that everything on the material plane, from rocks to puppies, has a certain type of energy surrounding it and flowing from it. If you can learn to recognize the unique energies of material things, then you can learn to influence them and to call upon them during your spell work, divination, and other magickal practices.

Hedge Magick

If you often find yourself "winging it," you might be a natural-born hedge magick practitioner. Hedge magick is magick that doesn't belong to any particular Pagan tradition and isn't exercised through a traditional formalized ritual. It doesn't follow any particular set of rules nor does it allow itself to be bound by tradition or conformity.

Hedge magick practitioners don't memorize spells off by heart, nor do they wait for the full moon to invoke spirits. Instead, their entire magickal practice revolves around the tenet that magick is most effective when it is both spontaneous and sincere. Anything highly ritualized is prone to losing its sincerity, this leads many hedge magick practitioners to shy away from covens and other Pagan groups that encourage or mandate several scripted magickal ceremonies.

Consequently, you'll need to get comfortable with crafting your own spells and getting used to making use of them when you feel the urge to do so (and not when it's most convenient for you) if you're planning on building your magickal repertoire on hedge magick.

Tools of the Trade

Hedge magick practitioners also often shun the ritualized use of Pagan tools. However, if you're not looking to turn your back on tradition altogether, learning how to use the tools of the trade can seriously improve the scope of your craft if you know how to use them correctly.

Symbolism is an integral part of many magickal practices. Most of the Pagan tools that are used during traditional rituals and ceremonies are nothing but an extension of the thread of symbolism that runs through all Pagan traditions. However, don't make the mistake of thinking that just because something is "only symbolic," that it's not powerful. Symbols are incredibly powerful in and of themselves because they allow us to express our intentions to the universe (and any deities who might be watching) in the simplest of ways. All magickal practices stem from the concept of intentionality; as a result of this, symbols are a natural amplifier for magick.

Wands

"The wand chooses the wizard, Mr. Potter." That's the phrase that comes to my mind when I hear the word 'wand.' Harry Potter and the wand salesman, Mr. Ollivander, are undoubtedly some of the most likable fictional wizards around but unfortunately, they are only fictional. Their depiction of wands is consequently only fictional too.

While it would be fantastic if wands could zap people and turn them into ferrets as they do in J.K. Rowling's wizarding world, that's not entirely how they work in reality. In the real world, wands serve as 'conductors' for the magickal abilities of whoever is wielding them. They can be used to direct magick but the jury's still out on whether they can be used to amplify it. With their amplification abilities under scrutiny, you can be relatively sure that you won't accidentally turn your aunt into a toad by waving one around, though you definitely could use one to direct your magick towards a certain spot on your body while you're conducting a healing spell.

Wands don't need to be made out of any particular material to be effective although wood has naturally remained popular regardless.

Candles

If you can't resist the urge to shop for Yankee Candles, you might as well capitalize on your waxy weakness by learning how to use candles to enhance your magickal practices.

The use of candles is naturally a form of elemental magick as they allow you to incorporate the element of fire into any number of spells, rituals, or ceremonies. Fire isn't the only symbolic attribute that they offer Pagans; the incredible variety of scents and colors that they come in add a whole new dimension to the ways that they can be used. There are several guides available on which color candles to use during which magickal rituals although most of them can easily be deduced by using a good dose of logic. Red candles are said to be good for love spells, black candles for necromancy or curses, yellow candles for protection spells, white candles for cleansing spells, and blue candles for binding spells.

When it comes to incorporating candles into your magickal practices, you essentially have two choices pertaining to how you're going to go about it. You can either take the hedge magick route and "wing it," using the types of candles that your 'gut' (or intuition) tells you are right, or you can take the traditional route and dedicate some time to reading up on which candles are traditionally used for which spells and rituals.

Daggers

In Pagan magickal practices, daggers are not used for stabbing things (preferably). Instead, they're usually employed as a kind of "wand replacement" during spells and ceremonies. They're particularly popular in the Wiccan community and as "wand replacements," they serve the same purpose, directing their wielders' magickal abilities in a more concentrated way than would otherwise be sent out into the world.

Daggers often have runes, sigils, or crystals imbued with their own magickal abilities included in their hilt or carved into their blade, allowing them to take on a lot more intentional energy than most wooden wands can take on. Silver daggers are also said to be handy in keeping malevolent entities at bay, while their wielder is communicating with the spirit world (if you're fortunate enough to be able to afford one).

Altars

The word 'altar' sounds pretty primitive, but many modern Pagans find a lot of joy in setting up one of their own. Most modern Pagan altars are a table or surface of some kind that the practitioner uses to store their tools (like crystals, daggers, candles, or wands) on. They are also often laden with trinkets of the Gods and Goddesses that the practitioner worships and sometimes even little offerings (like food or drink) to these deities. Altars are a great place to conduct magick from, when it's not possible to conduct it outside. Some practitioners even swear that the items that are laid out on the altar allow the practitioner standing before it, to tap into a larger magickal reserve.

Many Pagan practitioners decorate their altars to match the

point of the year that they're currently at (this is often based on the seasonal holidays laid out in the Wiccan Wheel of the Year). Others enjoy maintaining their altars by regularly adding new natural elements, like pretty flowers or oddly shaped rocks, to them to honor the ultimate driving force behind all Paganism: nature. At the end of the day, altars are a highly personal thing which means that every individual Pagan is tasked with creating the perfect altar for them. Unfortunately, this means that you won't be able to copy an altar straight off of Pinterest and expect the same results that you'd get from one that was crafted using your intuition.

The Rule of Three and Other Pitfalls of Magick

While it's wonderful to master the art of magick because it will allow you to protect yourself and others, influence reality and the material world to your benefit, and call upon the wisdom of spirits and other higher powers, it is not without its pitfalls.

The most prolific of these pitfalls is best described by the "Rule of Three." The Rule of Three states that whatever you send into the world through magick comes back to you threefold. In other words, if you bless others, you'll be blessed three times as much as the blessings you gave. Inversely, if you curse others, you can expect three times more misfortune than you imparted on them. It's important to keep the Rule of Three in mind during all of your magickal practices lest you unintentionally unleash harm upon yourself by wishing it upon others.

One of the most well-known dangers of magick pertains to communing with spirits. I'm sure most of us have watched a horror movie that's premise was that a group of friends (or a single simpleton) played with an Ouija board and accidentally unleashed a malevolent spirit or an ancient evil. There's a reason why this storyline is popular in Hollywood; it's because it's realistic. Magick practitioners are generally in universal agreement that a certain amount of caution needs to be taken when calling upon spirits or entities. Luckily, there are several simple steps that you can take to protect yourself (like casting a circle of salt around yourself before communing with the dead or only communicating with spirits who are known to you) that make it possible to continue with this Pagan tradition without having to worry about anything otherworldly attaching itself to you.

CHAPTER 7
RITUALS

Magick is usually the result of a Pagan ritual (either a personal ritual or a ritual that is prescribed by your chosen path). Rituals are one of the ways in which Pagans announce their intentions and wishes to the Universe (and to any other deities that may be listening). Some rituals, like the Calling the Corners ceremony, are highly formalized and follow a specific format, while others are more esoteric and are often largely created or conceptualized by the individual practitioner who employs them. In this chapter, we'll dive into the murky depths of ritual magick and examine the elements of Pagan rituals.

Regardless of the type of Pagan path that you're planning on journeying down, it's incredibly likely that you'll be expected to participate in a ritual or feel the need to conduct one to achieve a magickal goal at some point during your practice. For this reason, it's important to familiarize yourself with the basic principles that you'll need to understand and complete a ritual.

Calling the Corners (and the Role of the Elements)

Many Pagans believe that the best way to kick off any ritual is by Calling the Corners. This is a ceremony in and of itself that involves evoking the four magnetic directions on a compass, and their corresponding elements, as a way to involve the natural world in a spell, invocation, or blessing. North is associated with Earth, East with air, West with water, and South with fire. The majority of Pagans try to involve the elements in their spell work in some way and it makes total sense to do so. The world is made up of building blocks and in their simplest form, these building blocks can easily be described as water, earth, air, and fire. If you can manipulate these building blocks, or affect them in even the slightest of ways, the ripple effect could potentially change the material world as we know it.

Most Pagan practitioners believe that Calling the Corners is an integral part of being able to practice their craft safely not only because of the importance of the elements but also because doing so is said to drive away any malevolent energies or dark forces that might negatively affect any of the practitioner's magickal intentions or spell work. Calling the Corners' protective abilities is said to stem from the fact that these calls not only evoke the elements but also usually call upon their 'guardians' or corresponding deities (albeit, not always by name).

You'll need to cast a circle before commencing any spell work. A circle is a boundary that you create between yourself and the spirit world that serves to shield you from any uninvited energies, spirits, or deities. There are many different ways to cast a circle. The most popular method involves using a common kitchen condiment: salt. To cast a circle using it, you'll need a good handful of it (if not more). Once you've positioned yourself wherever it is that you're planning on conducting the Calling the Corners ceremony, you'll sprinkle it around you whilst uttering the following spell:

> "Salt of birth, salt of mirth, salt of hearth,
> Cleanse and sanctify this holy Earth.
> In this circle of protection and safety,
> As I mote it, so shall it be."

It's not uncommon for individual practitioners to create their own circle casting spells and rhymes based on their specific needs either. You're welcome to do so too, as long as you're careful to make your intention to cleanse the space clear. Some practitioners choose to repeat their circle casting chant a number of times before starting Calling the Corners.

Once you've cast a circle and you're ready to start Calling the Corners, you should walk around the circumference of it exactly three times before turning and facing North (you may need to keep a compass handy if you're not comfortable with finding North without it).

When you're facing North, you can start the ceremony. Just like the spell you use while casting a circle, the chant that you use to Call the Corners can be changed (and entirely rewritten) if you're comfortable doing so to make it suit your specific needs. Until you're comfortable with creating your own, you could make use of the following chant:

> "I call upon the watchtowers of the North,
> Solid as the Earth from which life springs forth.
> I call upon the watchtowers of the East,
> Omnipresent as the air that my lungs have released.

I call upon the watchtowers of the South,
Powerful as fire and the words from my mouth.
I call upon the watchtowers of the West,
Flow forth from me like water and thus be blessed."

Some Pagan Paths encourage their followers to repeat their Calling of the Corners chant three times before proceeding with any other spell work while others believe that performing it once is enough. You'll need to decide for yourself whether you think it should be conducted a couple of times or whether a single run-through is sufficient.

Pagan Practices and Procedures

Christians normally go to Church on Sundays (or say a prayer before bed), Muslims pray five times a day (making sure to face towards Mecca every single time) and fast during Ramadan, and Jewish people fast during Yom Kippur and consume a ritual meal during Pesach. Every single religion has its own practices. These practices are often fundamental to whatever belief the religion is centered on (in other words, they have to be conducted to keep a deity appeased or to ensure that it will offer you guidance and protection). Paganism is no different, although its 'rules' are naturally less stringent and practitioners are given a lot more free rein to determine how, when, and if they'll incorporate these practices into their belief systems.

Prayer

Most Pagans choose a handful of deities to observe and shape their everyday lives around them. These deities are often selected because the practitioner relates to them on a personal level. However, they're naturally expected to play a larger role than simply being likable. This role involves offering the same guidance and protection that followers of other religions expect from their deities. Prayer is how this guidance and protection is requested, so it's no surprise that most Pagan practitioners incorporate prayer into their belief systems too.

Pagan prayers usually aren't as formal as the prayers that are conducted by followers of Abrahamic religions. Many Pagans consider doing something that brings them closer to nature, like gardening or horseback riding, a prayer, others simply close their eyes, and ask their deity for help or intervention. You'll need to decide for yourself how you'd like to pray and to whom you'd like to pray.

Worship

Worship is another trait that most Pagan Paths share with quite a few mainstream religions. It's incredibly rare for Pagans to have any form of 'church service,' which means that Pagan worship is much less structured. Pagans are left to decide how they'd like to worship their chosen deities. Many enjoy worshiping them through song or dance while leaving 'offerings' (in the form of food, drinks, coins, pretty stones, or flowers) remains popular too. Offerings are often left on windowsills, in doorways, or on altars.

The purpose of worship is to build up a repertoire with your chosen deities. By working on fostering a relationship with them, you'll improve the chances that they'll be willing to assist you in your spell work, to be invoked, and to offer blessings or protections.

Cleansing

Cleansing is a religious practice that is uniquely Pagan. Pagans are keenly aware that the world is made up of positive and negative energy. Naturally, they normally only try to surround themselves with positive ones. Of course, this means that they had to find a way to drive out any negative energies that might be hanging around. Negative energies are believed to be responsible for everything from bad luck to depression, so it seems reasonable to want to get rid of them.

'Smudging' is probably the most popularized cleansing ritual. It involves brandishing a piece of burning sage and directing the smoke that rolls off of it into every corner of the room. Sage smoke is believed to drive out evil spirits and malevolent energies. Although it's a pretty nifty tool to have if your house is haunted, it is also said to be quite useful if you've had some personal trouble that you'd like to clear out of your space.

Other cleansing rituals involve sprinkling salt in window frames and doorways to keep negative energies from entering your home or using saltwater to anoint your home to force any evil spirits that might be present to leave.

Rituals for Beginners

Calling the Corners is just one Pagan ritual; there are hundreds (if not thousands) that haven't been mentioned in this book. Familiarizing yourself with all of them will likely take years, although that doesn't mean that you should avoid doing so. It can be incredibly rewarding and empowering to have various rituals in your arsenal, though it's always smart to familiarize yourself with the most basic ones first.

Blessing

Blessing rituals and ceremonies are common on most Pagan paths. Usually, they involve asking a specific deity to impart good fortune on you, although there are blessing ceremonies that evoke the entire pantheon of Gods and Goddesses that the individual practitioner worships (they're normally employed during rites of passage and marriage ceremonies).

The most simple blessing ritual is called, "Calling Upon The Spirit." It can be adapted to be used to kindly request a blessing from any deity and asks the deity not only to bless you but also to bless those that are important to you.

In short, it involves casting a circle and then kneeling in the middle of it while holding a bowl containing some kind of offering on your lap (it's advisable to do some research on the kind of offerings that your chosen deity prefers). Once in this position, you'll utter the following spell:

> "[Name of deity] I call you down to the world of men
> To beg for guidance and help once again.
> Bless me and anoint me as I bless others,
> And guide the spirits of my sisters and brothers.
> Lend me a hand when I fumble and fall,
> And be with my friends and family, one and all.
> Make me wise, brave, kind, and true,
> So that I may grow even closer to you."

Once you've completed the spell, you'll get up and place the bowl of offerings in the center of the circle that you had cast earlier. You'll need to leave it there for one day and one night before it's advisable to clear it or clean it up. Don't be disheartened if the offerings look untouched! The symbolism behind offerings matters more to most deities than actually being able to consume or take possession of them.

Binding

Bindings are uniquely Pagan. Essentially, they're rituals (or rather, ritual spell work) that work to inhibit a certain person from committing a specific act or deed. They're often used in conjunction with protection rituals to shield a practitioner from harm that someone intends to inflict upon them.

Naturally, binding rituals need to be changed or adapted to suit whichever action they're intended to stop someone from committing, although they all take on more or less the same structure.

One of the most popular binding rituals requires the use of a piece of string and a candle. To conduct this ritual, you'll need to cast a circle and kneel inside of it with a lit candle in front of you and a piece of rope in one of your hands. You'll then need to recite the following spell, tying a knot in the piece of rope after every line of it.

"[Name of person] I bind thee.
I bind thee from [action you'd like to stop the person from doing.]
As the knots in this rope you're bound to me.
As I mote it, so shall it be."

Once you've recited the spell, you should dangle the knotted rope above the candle, allowing it to catch flame and partially (or entirely) burn away. Make sure to have a nonflammable bowl or plate nearby to place the burning piece of rope on to avoid scorching your fingertips.

Protection

Pagan protection rituals involve calling upon a specific deity to ask them to shield you from harm. Most Pagan Paths prescribe their own specific protection rituals, although there are a couple that seem to be relatively generic. The simplest of these requires that you create a mixture of salt and water beforehand. Once you've concocted it, you'll need to cast a circle and kneel in the center of it with your salt-water mixture nearby. You'll then need to recite the following spell:

"[Your chosen deity] although fear and death hound me, I call

upon thee.
Lend me the protection that I lack and arm me with your weaponry.
Shield me from those who seek to do me harm or see me fail,
And have your wishes, through me, your servant, prevail."

After reciting the spell, you'll need to wash your hands, feet, and forehead with the salt-water mixture and allow them to dry before leaving the circle.

CHAPTER 8
WHEEL OF THE YEAR

The "Wheel of the Year" is even more important than the actual calendar is to most modern Pagans. It was derived from a number of folk traditions and only became known in its current form in the twentieth century. It is made up of eight separate holy days; their dates are determined by the sun's position in relation to the earth. The seasonal nature of these holy days is exactly what makes them so special to those on nature-centric paths.

Important Dates on the Wheel of the Year

As mentioned earlier, the dates on the Wheel of the Year are determined by the seasons. Naturally, this means that the Wheel of the Year's holy day's dates are different in the Northern Hemisphere than they are in the Southern

Hemisphere. It's important to note this difference to ensure that you're not following a version of the Wheel of the Year that is incompatible with your geographical location.

Yule

Yule is celebrated between the twentieth and the twenty-third of December in the Northern Hemisphere and between the twentieth and the twenty-third of June in the Southern Hemisphere. It is essentially a celebration that is centered upon the occurrence of the winter solstice, a time when the Earth starts regaining its fertility and the natural world starts coming back to life.

Yule is celebrated in many different ways, although most celebrations involve a gathering of family and/or friends, a feast, and the giving of gifts.

Samhain

Samhain is the holiday that Halloween is based on. It is

celebrated on the first of November in the Northern Hemisphere and the first of May in the Southern Hemisphere. The ancient Gaelic Pagans used to observe it as a harvest festival, making the time of the year when they'd start stripping their crops and slaughtering any animals that they didn't plan on keeping through winter.

The ancient Gaelic Pagans believed that the veil between the spirit world and the world of the living was particularly thin during Samhain, allowing the dead to wander through the streets. Most modern Pagans make use of Samhain to remember and honor family and friends who have passed away. Some Pagans even go as far as invoking or inviting their dead friends or relatives to the festivities.

Lughnasadh

Lughnasadh is also often called 'Lammas.' It is celebrated on the first of August in the Northern Hemisphere and on the first of February in the Southern Hemisphere. It is a minor harvest festival that is mostly celebrated by Pagans on a Wiccan Path.

The Ancient Celts devoted Lughnasadh to the worship of one of their main deities, Lugh. Over the years, changes in tradition led to the holiday being referred to as 'Lammas.' Lammas specifically marks the harvest date for grain. Consequently, it's known as the "bread holiday." Modern Pagans often celebrate it by baking a loaf of bread as an offering to their chosen deity.

Mabon

Mabon marks the end of the harvest season. It is celebrated between the twenty-first and the twenty-fourth of September in the Northern hemisphere and between the twenty-first and the twenty-fourth of March in the Southern Hemisphere.

Hundreds of years ago, Pagans celebrated it by sharing fruits, grain, and vegetables from their harvest and meat from any animals that they may have slaughtered with their neighbors and friends. In modernity, it is one of the lesser celebrated occasions. However, when it is celebrated, it is celebrated with a feast that is often accompanied by the giving of gifts.

Litha

Litha marks the summer solstice. It is celebrated between the nineteenth and the twenty-third of June in the Northern Hemisphere and between the nineteenth and twenty-third of December in the Southern Hemisphere.

It is celebrated in modernity in much the same way that it was celebrated in antiquity: through dancing, singing, and the building of bonfires. For Pagans, it's somewhat of a last hurrah before winter comes around and confines them to their homes for days on end again. Some ancient Pagan traditions involved leaping over bonfires for good luck and building elaborate wooden effigies to burn during Litha.

Beltane

Beltane is also often referred to as "May Ever" or "May Day." It is celebrated on the first of May in the Northern Hemisphere and on the first of November in the Southern Hemisphere. Beltane is celebrated to honor what most Pagans believe to be the first day of summer.

Thousands of years ago, Irish and Scottish Pagans observed this holiday as a day on which their deities were particularly inclined to grant blessings. They utilized this benefit by blessing as many things as they could. To do so, they built two large ritual bonfires and asked their deities to bless anything that passes through them. They then proceeded to herd all of their cattle, pets, and family members through the gap between the two fires. In modernity, some Pagans still observe this tradition while others simply light candles around their homes and ask their deities to bless whoever passes past these.

Ostara

Ostara marks the spring equinox. It is celebrated between the nineteenths and the twenty-second of March in the Northern Hemisphere and between the nineteenth and the twenty-second of October in the Southern Hemisphere. The ancient observation of Ostara led to the modern Christian version of Easter which means that it was, and often still is, celebrated in much the same way.

Ostara doesn't only mark the spring equinox, it's a fertility festival too and is suitably commemorated with a number of fertility symbols like chocolate eggs and bunnies. Much like Christians, Pagans often celebrate Ostara by hiding treats around their homes and gardens and sending their children (or spirited adults) to search for them.

Imbolc

Imbolc is used to celebrate the beginning of Spring. It is celebrated on the second of February in the Northern Hemisphere and on the second of August in the Southern Hemisphere.

Historically, it was celebrated by the Celts by sacrificing ewes to the Goddess Brigid. In modernity, Pagans celebrate it by spring cleaning, clearing their homes of spiritual and physical clutter, and by making pledges or dedications for the upcoming year (much like New Year's resolutions).

Personal Seasons

The eight holidays that are observed on the Wheel of the Year aren't the only seasons that are important to and celebrated by modern Pagans, personal seasons are just as revered. A "personal season" is a pivotal period in anyone's life. Examples of personal seasons are marriage, becoming a parent, reaching puberty, death, and coming of age. These personal seasons can be celebrated in an individualized way by involving whichever deity (or deities) the practitioner honors or in a more formalized way by following the specific rites of their chosen path.

CHAPTER 9
CONTINUING YOUR SPIRITUAL JOURNEY

Most religious systems posit that you need to do a little more than just reading their religious texts before you can consider yourself an expert on them. Paganism is no different. If you've decided that you feel called to some kind of Paganism, you'll likely spend the next couple of decades studying it and learning everything that there is to know about it. Before you can truly devote yourself to your craft, there are a couple of questions that you have to ask yourself, the most important of which is, "Which Pagan Path am I going to follow?"

Now that you have a relatively good idea of what modern Paganism is all about, you should start considering which Pagan path you'd like to follow. There's no right answer to the question of, "Which path is the best?" The best path for you is the one that resonates with you most, that's deities you relate to, and that's practices are in line with your moral code.

The following quiz should give you a better idea of which path seems to be best suited to you, although you shouldn't make your choice based solely on its results. Add up the results from the quiz below and compare them to the key after the quiz to see which path suits your personality!

Quiz: Which Pagan Path is Right for Me?

- When I'm spending time with my friends, I'm likely to…
    A) Be the life of the party. I'll be the first on the dance floor and the last to leave.
    B) Spend my time telling stories from my life and listening to the stories of others.
    C) Try to see if I can out-drink or out-party everybody else at the party. I'm capable of turning anything into a competitive endeavor!
    D) Be sitting in a quiet corner somewhere with my closest companions, discussing politics, current events, and philosophy.

- When I have some free time (or 'me' time) you'll find me…
    A) Spending time with my friends or family.
    B) Outside enjoying nature (preferably in a primordial forest)
    C) Engaging in a sport or other competitive pursuit.
    D) Making art or playing music.

- You find $100 on the floor in a shopping mall. You immediately...
  A) Spend it on your friends or family.
  B) Shove it in your pocket. Finders keepers!
  C) Hand it over to a security guard, although you keep $20 of it as a finder's fee.
  D) Hand it over to a security guard (every cent of it) with exact details on the position and location that you found it in. You offer to help search for its rightful owner.

- You go to the pet shop to buy a new fluffy/furry/scaly/feathery companion. You come home with a...
  A) Black cat.
  B) A raven or a crow.
  C) A dog.
  D) A snake.

- Someone backs-up into your car in the parking lot. You watch as it happens and instantly react by...
  A) Forgiving the driver who backed-up into you and trying to befriend them. Maybe they're having a bad day already and you wouldn't want to make it any worse.
  B) Confronting the driver. You're not above a physical confrontation either.

C) Confronting the driver and demanding his insurance information. You're not looking for a fight but you have a firm sense of justice, and it would only be right for their insurance to pay for your damage.

D) Pretending that you didn't see it. You don't want to cause a scene in public, plus you don't mind having your insurance cover the damage.

- You miss the deadline for a project that your boss asked you to complete. You react by...

    A) Buying your boss lunch and telling them that you've missed the deadline while they're mid-bite.

    B) Lying about it. When the boss asks whether it has been done, you say, "yes." You quickly complete and submit the project during lunch before anyone's even aware of the fact that it's late.

    C) Telling your boss that the project is going to be a little late. However, you assure them that it's because you're about to produce the best project that they've ever had the privilege of laying eyes on.

    D) Telling your boss that the project is going to be late while apologizing profusely. You stay at work after hours to get it done that evening.

- Your significant other tells you that they no longer want to be in a relationship with you. You...

    A) Immediately burst into tears and beg them to stay.

B) Block them on all of your social media accounts and start pretending that they never existed.
C) Reply courteously and spend the rest of the night partying with other eligible single people at a bar, club, or similar establishment.
D) Reply courteously and spend the next couple of days quietly lamenting your loss before making peace with it and moving on.

Quiz Key: Interpret Your Results

Tally up how many As, Bs, Cs, and Ds you got on the test. You'll use whichever of those letters you got the most of to determine which Pagan Path seems to suit you best. Refer back to Chapter Four if you need to refresh your memory when it comes to the different types of Pagan Paths.

If You Got Mostly As

If you got mostly As, you'll likely find yourself drawn to Wicca. Wicca offers its practitioners the chance to practice their craft alongside like-minded individuals, which makes it the ideal path for more sociable Pagans. Wicca is also perfect for people who are interested in learning to do magick to aid others and to protect themselves.

If You Got Mostly Bs

If you got mostly Bs, you should consider Ásatrú or Odinism. Both of these Paths can be practiced alone or in a group, making it perfect for introverts and extroverts alike. Ásatrú and Odinism practitioners do not prescribe to traditional Christian values. This makes both of these paths attractive to those who question the black-and-white morality that is so often forced upon people.

If You Got Mostly Cs

If you got mostly Cs, Roman Neopaganism or Stregheria are likely good fits for you. Both of these paths are ideal for Pagans who want to use their magickal abilities to advance their personal lives, finances, and relationships. Regardless of their incredibly enabling natures, these paths also boast set moral codes that serve to guide their followers' actions and decisions.

If You Got Mostly Ds

If you got mostly Ds, Hellenism might be just the Pagan Path for you! Hellenists have strong communal values and, just like the Greek philosophers who first prescribed to this type of belief system, are quite stoic. This Pagan Path is a fantastic fit for the less flamboyant Pagans out there who are more interested in the philosophies behind Paganism than they are in practicing magick.

CHAPTER 10
CONTINUING YOUR PAGAN EDUCATION

Reading this book is a fantastic start to your Pagan education, but it certainly shouldn't end on the last page. If you're truly serious about devoting yourself to a Pagan Path, you'll need to learn as much about it as is physically possible. Knowledge is power, after all. Most Pagan Paths don't have a singular religious text or even an easily accessible set of religious texts, this means that studying them can be a bit trickier than studying Abrahamic religions is.

Fortunately, there are several sources that you can consult at the beginning of your Pagan journey that will help you to start your education. This chapter will serve to guide you in choosing texts to study to improve your understanding of Pagan practices, traditions, beliefs, and rituals.

How Do I Continue My Education?

At the beginning of your Pagan journey, you should try to devote an hour or two every day to improving your knowledge of your chosen Pagan Path. It would be silly to describe yourself as a devotee to any specific Path if you know very little of it. For this reason, it's important to spend a fair amount of time familiarizing yourself with its beliefs and practices. Learning about the different Pagan Paths and their varying attributes will also ultimately help you to decide which Pagan belief system resonates with you most.

Books

The printed word remains one of the best ways to improve your knowledge on any subject. This is true for Paganism too.

If you're looking for an academic analysis on the Pagan beliefs in modern America, Margot Adler's *Drawing Down The Moon* is the place to start. In this book, Adler describes the practices and beliefs of a number of modern Pagan sects that are currently active in the USA. She's also not scared to take a look at some of their darker practices and beliefs, which makes this source an honest reflection of the reality of practicing in a coven or group.

Of course, not everyone's interested in joining a coven or other type of Pagan group. Many Pagans prefer practicing alone. There's no shame in being a solitary practitioner, although it does mean that you'll need to adapt certain formalized Pagan rituals that normally call for a group of practitioners to suit your needs. Scott Cunningham's *Wicca: A Guide For The Solitary Practitioner* is a fantastic resource to consult if you're looking for guidance on how to do so.

If the magickal aspect of Paganism is particularly important to you and you're looking to empower or enrich yourself through spells, you should probably pick up a copy of Raymond Buckland's *Complete Book of Witchcraft*. In this book, Buckland shares a number of structured exercises that are intended to help the healer hone their natural magickal abilities.

The more magick you're capable of performing, the more moral conundrums you're likely to encounter. Luckily, there are a number of Pagan books that have been written to help you navigate the ethics of Paganism and magick. The best of these is Phyllis Curott's *Witch Crafting*. As a constitutional lawyer, Phyllis approaches the morals of magick and influencing the material world through the Gods and Goddesses with the steely resolve of a seasoned attorney.

YouTube Channels

If you're struggling to carve out enough time every day to spend hours and hours reading Pagan books, you might want to consider subscribing to a couple of Pagan YouTube channels instead.

One of the best channels to subscribe to is called *The Witch of Wonderlust* ('wonderlust' being a clever amalgamation of the words 'wonder' and 'wanderlust'). This channel is run by a woman who is known only as 'Olivia.' It grants the viewers unique insight into how her coven operates. She's also more than happy to share her magickal knowledge with her viewers by teaching them the spells and rituals that have worked for her. Some of her more imaginative content includes segments like "Tipsy Tarot," during which she attempts to read tarot cards while under the influence of copious amounts of wine.

If you're interested in learning how to practice herbal magick or would like to improve your knowledge of medicinal plants, you should subscribe to *Gather Thyme*. This channel is run by a woman known as 'Genevieve.' Her videos serve to educate her viewers on the magickal and medicinal uses of a number of different herbs. She explains her craft in a way that's easy to understand, this makes her content easily digestible for beginners.

The most popular YouTube channel among those seeking knowledge on some of magick's darker practices is called *The Lady Grave Dancer*. This channel does not shy away from touching on topics like necromancy, although it has a wide enough variety that it also covers elements of kitchen magick (and even includes a delicious recipe for sweet rose biscuits) and divination.

Blogs

If you'd like to hold off on spending any money on purchasing books on Paganism until you're certain that you've chosen a Path that you're going to stick with, you should consider consulting blogs alongside the YouTube channels that were mentioned above.

Witchesandpagans.com should be your first port of call if you're looking for online Pagan literature. It is a platform that hosts a pretty impressive number of blogs that are written and posted by a large group of individual pagan practitioners. The variety that this blog offers means that it has something for everyone.

Another conglomerate that is worth a read is called *Wildhunt.org*. This blog is run by numerous Pagans from all around the world. Its global nature means that it'll offer you insight into how Paganism is practiced in countries other than your own. This exchange of information is not only valuable because you might learn how to perform a new magick spell or two, it's also valuable because it gives its readers a chance to broaden their horizons by introducing them to a variety of different world views and Pagan belief systems.

If you're looking for information on how to cleanse your home using crystals or how to heal your loved ones using herbs, you might want to consider consulting *Goodwitcheshomestead.com*. This blog touches on a number of magickal practices (mostly protective or cleansing in nature) without delving into anything darker that might deter some practitioners.

If you're more into divination, *Thehoodwitch.com* is a good option. This channel contains quite a bit of information on tarot card divination. It is presented in an entertaining and humorous way that makes it seem relatable, inviting, and unthreatening.

CONCLUSION

Armed with the knowledge imparted on you during this book and with the wisdom you'll gain from some of the sources mentioned in Chapter Ten, you'll be a fully-fledged Pagan in no time. Being a Pagan means joining the ranks of hundreds of thousands (if not millions) of your ancestors that walked a similar path with the Old Gods and upheld identical values and beliefs. Every tradition that you'll participate in as a Pagan is an heirloom passed down to you by those that came before you, every ceremony is a covenant with the Earth, and every spell a love song to a deity. Paganism, in all of its shapes and forms, is undoubtedly beautiful. It's no wonder that ever more people seem to be drawn to it.

Paganism will change your life for the better. Unlike many other belief systems, Paganism will welcome you with open arms just as you are, regardless of what you look like, your gender, your sexual preferences, or your political identity. As long as you're on a nature-centric path, there will always be a community of like-minded individuals who have your back and who will care for you if you let them. Of course, Paganism also allows its practitioners to practice privately and in secret. Unlike many mainstream religions, Pagan Paths do not shun their adherents who feel that they have to be closeted in their practice of the craft for whatever reason. Pagan deities do not demand to be worshiped in public, which means that you're under no obligation to reveal your beliefs to your family and friends if you do not feel comfortable doing so.

Whatever first drew you to Paganism is rather irrelevant, but now that you're here you can rest assured in the knowledge that you've found a community (and deities) that will love you for who you are, instead of for what they perceive or expect you to be.

Thank you so much for reading this book. I hope you found it useful as an introduction to Paganism. I'd appreciate any feedback, and please do consider leaving a review.

REFERENCES

7 Ancient Pagan Gods We Still Love Today. (n.d.). www.beliefnet.com. https://www.beliefnet.com/entertainment/7-ancient-pagan-gods-we-still-love-today.aspx

7 Signs You Are a Pagan. (n.d.). Exemplore. https://exemplore.com/paganism/Are-You-a-Pagan-7-Signs-That-Pagansim-is-Your-Path

10 Celtic Deities You Should Know. (n.d.). Learn Religions. https://www.learnreligions.com/gods-of-the-celts-2561711

11 things to know about the present day practice of Ásatrú, the ancient religion of the Vikings. (n.d.). Icelandmag. Retrieved August 14, 2020, from https://icelandmag.is/article/11-things-know-about-present-day-practice-asatru-ancient-religion-vikings

Angel. (n.d.). In *Pixabay.com*. https://cdn.pixabay.com/photo/2018/04/09/10/07/woman-3303696_960_720.jpg

Animal Magick. (n.d.). In *Pixabay.com*. https://cdn.pixabay.com/photo/2018/03/27/10/49/portrait-3265622_960_720.jpg

Asatru Alliance | Questions and Answers about Asatru. (n.d.). Www.Asatru.Org. https://www.asatru.org/aboutasatru.php

Aztec. (n.d.). In *Pixabay.com*.
>   https://cdn.pixabay.com/photo/2013/10/13/17/50/aztec-195134_960_720.jpg

Beginners' Guide to Paganism, Wicca, Witchcraft, Shamanism. (n.d.). www.sorcerers-apprentice.co.uk.
>   http://www.sorcerers-apprentice.co.uk/staroff2.htm

Beginner's Tips for Getting Started in Paganism. (n.d.). Learn Religions. Retrieved August 14, 2020, from https://www.learnreligions.com/getting-started-as-a-pagan-or-wiccan-2561838

Blood Magick. (n.d.). In *Pixabay.com*.
>   https://cdn.pixabay.com/photo/2017/04/10/06/11/glass-2217664_960_720.jpg

Bridesmaids. (n.d.). In *Pixabay.com*.
>   https://cdn.pixabay.com/photo/2020/07/22/00/16/bride-5427660_960_720.jpg

Candles. (n.d.). In *Pixabay.com*.
>   https://cdn.pixabay.com/photo/2017/04/12/07/46/tea-lights-2223898_960_720.jpg

Celtic Gods. (n.d.). Mythopedia.
>   https://mythopedia.com/celtic-mythology/gods/

CELTIC GODS & GODDESSES – Celtic Life International. (n.d.). https://celticlifeintl.com/celtic-gods-goddesses/

Cleansing. (n.d.). In *Unsplash.com*.
>   https://images.unsplash.com/photo-1520285793272-209a2fb209ba?ixlib=rb-

1.2.1&ixid=eyJhcHBfaWQiOjEyMDd9&auto=format
&fit=crop&w=750&q=80

Crystal Magick. (n.d.). In *Pixabay.com*.
https://cdn.pixabay.com/photo/2016/09/21/20/24/crystal-1685590_960_720.jpg

Diana. (n.d.). In *Pixabay.com*.
https://cdn.pixabay.com/photo/2014/10/20/15/28/diana-495410_960_720.jpg

Easter. (n.d.). In *Pixabay.com*.
https://cdn.pixabay.com/photo/2014/11/23/10/49/rabbit-542554_960_720.jpg

Greek Mythology. (2018, August 21). HISTORY.
https://www.history.com/topics/ancient-history/greek-mythology

Guide to Paganism – Religion Media Centre. (n.d.).
https://religionmediacentre.org.uk/factsheets/paganism/

Halloween. (n.d.). In *Pixabay.com*.
https://cdn.pixabay.com/photo/2017/10/31/15/16/halloween-2905531_960_720.jpg

Lady Justice. (n.d.). In *Pixabay.com*.
https://cdn.pixabay.com/photo/2017/02/12/14/00/justice-2060093_960_720.jpg

List of Deities. (n.d.). WikiPagan.
https://pagan.wikia.org/wiki/List_of_Deities

Magical tools in Wicca. (2020, July 10). Wikipedia. https://en.wikipedia.org/wiki/Magical_tools_in_Wicca

Meet the Gods and Goddesses of Paganism. (n.d.). Learn Religions. https://www.learnreligions.com/pagan-gods-and-goddesses-2561985

modernnorseheathen. (2017, June 21). *Heathenry for Beginners.* Modern Norse Heathen. https://modernnorseheathen.wordpress.com/2017/06/21/heathenry-for-beginners/

Moon, B. the. (2020, February 14). *The Art of Ritual: Calling the Quarters.* Beneath the Moon. https://www.patheos.com/blogs/beneaththemoon/2020/02/the-art-of-ritual-calling-the-quarters/

Odinism. (n.d.). Odinism and Asatru: Basic Facts. https://www.odinism.net/

Oracle Girl | Witch. (n.d.). In *Pixabay*. https://cdn.pixabay.com/photo/2017/03/10/23/13/oracle-girl-2133976_960_720.jpg

Pagan Altar. (n.d.). In *Pixabay.com*. https://cdn.pixabay.com/photo/2018/02/06/00/29/candle-3133631_960_720.jpg

Pagan Funerals: Rites, Prayers & What to Expect | Cake Blog. (n.d.). www.joincake.com. https://www.joincake.com/blog/pagan-funeral/

Pagan Rituals and Beliefs. (n.d.). SchoolWorkHelper. https://schoolworkhelper.net/pagan-rituals-and-beliefs/

Paganism for Beginners. (2020). Catanna.Com. http://www.catanna.com/paganism101.htm

Poseidon. (n.d.). In *Pixabay.com*. https://cdn.pixabay.com/photo/2016/02/09/22/33/poseidon-1190564_960_720.jpg

Prayer. (n.d.). In *Pixabay.com*. https://cdn.pixabay.com/photo/2017/12/30/13/26/fog-3050078_960_720.jpg

Rites and Ceremonies. (n.d.). Www.Patheos.Com. https://www.patheos.com/library/pagan/ritual-worship-devotion-symbolism/rites-and-ceremonies

Samhain. (n.d.). In *Pixabay.com*. https://cdn.pixabay.com/photo/2016/11/29/09/11/candle-1868640_960_720.jpg

Seddon, J. A. and K. (2004, May 1). *Egyptian Paganism for Beginners*. Llewellyn Worldwide. https://www.llewellyn.com/journal/article/613

Stregheria.com - The Home of Authentic Italian Witchcraft. (n.d.). www.stregheria.com. http://www.stregheria.com/

The 12 Gods and Goddesses of Pagan Rome. (2015). History Hit. https://www.historyhit.com/the-gods-and-goddesses-of-pagan-rome/

Thor. (n.d.). In *Pixabay.com*.
>https://cdn.pixabay.com/photo/2018/07/12/22/25/statue-3534492_960_720.jpg

Top 10 Ancient Roman Gods. (2019, February 8). AncientHistoryLists. https://www.ancienthistorylists.com/rome-history/top-10-ancient-roman-gods/

Twitter, T. (n.d.). *8 Traditions in Modern Paganism.* Learn Religions. https://www.learnreligions.com/best-known-pagan-paths-2562554

View Of Self. (n.d.). In *Pixabay.com*. https://cdn.pixabay.com/photo/2018/01/15/07/52/woman-3083390_960_720.jpg

What Are the Different Pagan Religions? (n.d.). Www.Beliefnet.Com. https://www.beliefnet.com/faiths/pagan-and-earth-based/what-are-the-different-pagan-religions.aspx

What Do Pagans Do? (n.d.). Pluralism.Org. https://pluralism.org/what-do-pagans-do

What is a Pagan? What is Paganism? (n.d.). Wicca Living. Retrieved August 14, 2020, from https://wiccaliving.com/what-is-paganism/

White Skull Conclusion. (n.d.). In *Unsplash.com*. https://images.unsplash.com/photo-1573682911645-1cdda2ef7b14?ixlib=rb-1.2.1&ixid=eyJhcHBfaWQiOjEyMDd9&auto=format&fit=crop&w=1500&q=80

Winters, R. (n.d.). *The True Meaning of Paganism.* Www.Ancient-Origins.Net. https://www.ancient-origins.net/myths-legends/true-meaning-paganism-002306

Witches Hat On Chair. (n.d.). In *Pixabay.com.* https://cdn.pixabay.com/photo/2018/10/10/15/09/halloween-3737488_960_720.jpg

Yule. (n.d.). In *Pixabay.com.* https://cdn.pixabay.com/photo/2019/12/03/07/34/gift-4669449_960_720.jpg

www.ingramcontent.com/pod-product-compliance
Lightning Source LLC
LaVergne TN
LVHW012109070526
838202LV00056B/5682